ON DREAMS

By SIGMUND FREUD

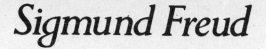

Sigmund Freud

ON
DREAMS

TRANSLATED AND EDITED BY
James Strachey

WITH A BIOGRAPHICAL
INTRODUCTION BY
Peter Gay

W·W·NORTON & COMPANY
New York · London

ISBN-13: 978-0-393-00144-0
ISBN-10: 0-393-00144-X

W. W. Norton & Company, Inc. is also the publisher of The Standard
Edition of the Complete Psychological Works of Sigmund Freud.

W. W. Norton & Company, Inc.
500 Fifth Avenue, New York, N.Y. 10110
www.wwnorton.com

W. W. Norton & Company Ltd.
Castle House, 75/76 Wells Street, London W1T 3QT

PRINTED IN THE UNITED STATES OF AMERICA

567890

Contents

SIGMUND FREUD: A BRIEF LIFE

by Peter Gay

It was Freud's fate, as he observed not without pride, to "agitate the sleep of mankind." Half a century after his death, it seems clear that he succeeded far better than he expected, though in ways he would not have appreciated. It is commonplace but true that we all speak Freud now, correctly or not. We casually refer to oedipal conflicts and sibling rivalry, narcissism and Freudian slips. But before we can speak that way with authority, we must read his writings attentively. They repay reading, with dividends.

Sigmund Freud was born on May 6, 1856, in the small Moravian town of Freiberg.[1] His father, Jacob Freud, was an impecunious merchant; his mother, Amalia, was handsome, self-assertive, and young—twenty years her husband's junior and his third wife. Jacob Freud had two sons from his first marriage who were about Amalia Freud's age and lived nearby. One of these half brothers had a son, John, who, though Sigmund Freud's nephew, was older than his uncle.

---

[1]His given names were Sigismund Schlomo, but he never used his middle name and, after experimenting with the shorter form for some time, definitively adopted the first name Sigmund—on occasion relapsing into the original formulation—in the early 1870s, when he was a medical student at the University of Vienna. Freiberg, now in Czechoslovakia, bears the Czech name "Pribor."

Freud's family constellation, then, was intricate enough to puzzle the clever and inquisitive youngster. Inquisitiveness, the natural endowment of children, was particularly marked in him. Life would provide ample opportunity to satisfy it.

In 1860, when Freud was almost four, he moved with his family to Vienna, then a magnet for many immigrants. This was the opening phase of the Hapsburg Empire's liberal era. Jews, only recently freed from onerous taxes and humiliating restrictions on their property rights, professional choices, and religious practices, could realistically harbor hopes for economic advancement, political participation, and a measure of social acceptance. This was the time, Freud recalled, when "every industrious Jewish school boy carried a Cabinet Minister's portfolio in his satchel."[2] The young Freud was encouraged to cultivate high ambitions. As his mother's first-born and a family favorite, he secured, once his family could afford it, a room of his own. He showed marked gifts from his first school days, and in his secondary school, or Gymnasium, he was first in his class year after year.

In 1873, at seventeen, Freud entered the University of Vienna. He had planned to study law, but, driven on by what he called his "greed for knowledge," instead matriculated in the faculty of medicine, intending to embark, not on a conventional career as a physician, but on philosophical-scientific investigations that might solve some of the great riddles that fascinated him. He found his work in physiology and neurology so absorbing that he did not take his degree until 1881.

A brilliant researcher, he cultivated the habit of close observation and the congenial stance of scientific skepticism. He was privileged to work under professors with inter-

---

[2] *The Interpretation of Dreams* (1900), *SE* IV, 193.

national reputations, almost all German imports and tough-minded positivists who disdained metaphysical speculations about, let alone pious explanations of, natural phenomena. Even after Freud modified their theories of the mind—in essence barely disguised physiological theories—he recalled his teachers with unfeigned gratitude. The most memorable of them, Ernst Brücke, an illustrious physiologist and a civilized but exacting taskmaster, confirmed Freud's bent as an unbeliever. Freud had grown up with no religious instruction at home, came to Vienna University as an atheist, and left it as an atheist—with persuasive scientific arguments.

In 1882, on Brücke's advice, Freud reluctantly left the laboratory to take a lowly post at the Vienna General Hospital. The reason was romantic: in April, he had met Martha Bernays, a slender, attractive young woman from northern Germany visiting one of his sisters, and fallen passionately in love. He was soon secretly engaged to her, but too poor to establish the respectable bourgeois household that he and his fiancée thought essential. It was not until September 1886, some five months after opening his practice in Vienna, with the aid of wedding gifts and loans from affluent friends, that the couple could marry. Within nine years, they had six children, the last of whom, Anna, grew up to be her father's confidante, secretary, nurse, disciple, and representative, and an eminent psychoanalyst in her own right.

Before his marriage, from October 1885 to February 1886, Freud worked in Paris with the celebrated French neurologist Jean-Martin Charcot, who impressed Freud with his bold advocacy of hypnosis as an instrument for healing medical disorders, and no less bold championship of the thesis (then quite unfashionable) that hysteria is an ailment to which men are susceptible no less than women.

Charcot, an unrivaled observer, stimulated Freud's growing interest in the theoretical and therapeutic aspects of mental healing. Nervous ailments became Freud's specialty, and in the 1890s, as he told a friend, psychology became his tyrant. During these years he founded the psychoanalytic theory of mind.

He had intriguing if somewhat peculiar help. In 1887, he had met a nose-and-throat specialist from Berlin, Wilhelm Fliess, and rapidly established an intimate friendship with him. Fliess was the listener the lonely Freud craved: an intellectual gambler shocked at no idea, a propagator of provocative (at times fruitful) theories, an enthusiast who fed Freud ideas on which he could build. For over a decade, Fliess and Freud exchanged confidential letters and technical memoranda, meeting occasionally to explore their subversive notions. And Freud was propelled toward the discovery of psychoanalysis in his practice: his patients proved excellent teachers. He was increasingly specializing in women suffering from hysteria, and, observing their symptoms and listening to their complaints, he found that, though a good listener, he did not listen carefully enough. They had much to tell him.

In 1895, Freud and his fatherly friend Josef Breuer, a thriving, generous internist, published *Studies on Hysteria*, assigning Breuer's former patient "Anna O." pride of place. She had furnished fascinating material for intimate conversations between Breuer and Freud, and was to become, quite against her—and Breuer's—will, the founding patient of psychoanalysis. She demonstrated to Freud's satisfaction that hysteria originates in sexual malfunctioning and that symptoms can be talked away.

The year 1895 was decisive for Freud in other ways. In July, Freud managed to analyze a dream, his own, fully. He would employ this dream, known as "Irma's injection," as a model for psychoanalytic dream interpretation when he published it, some four years later, in his *Interpretation of Dreams.* In the fall, he drafted, but neither completed nor published, what was later called the Project for a Scientific Psychology. It anticipated some of his fundamental theories yet serves as a reminder that Freud had been deeply enmeshed in the traditional physiological interpretation of mental events.

Increasingly Freud was offering psychological explanations for psychological phenomena. In the spring of 1896, he first used the fateful name, "psychoanalysis." Then in October his father died; "the most important event," he recalled a dozen years later, "the most poignant loss, of a man's life."[3] It supplied a powerful impetus toward psychoanalytic theorizing, stirring Freud to his unprecedented self-analysis, more systematic and thoroughgoing than the frankest autobiographer's self-probing. In the next three or four years, as he labored over his "Dream book," new discoveries crowded his days. But first he had to jettison the "seduction theory" he had championed for some time. It held that *every* neurosis results from premature sexual activity, mainly child molestation, in childhood.[4] Once freed from this far-reaching but improbable theory, Freud could appreciate the share of fantasies in mental life, and discover the Oedipus complex, that universal family triangle.

Freud's *Interpretation of Dreams* was published in November 1899.[5] It treated all dreams as wish fulfillments,

---

[3]Ibid., xxvi.

[4]Freud never claimed that sexual abuse does not exist. He had patients who he knew had not imagined the assaults they reported. All he abandoned when he abandoned the seduction theory was the sweeping claim that only the rape of a child, whether a boy or a girl, by a servant, an older sibling, or a classmate, could be the *only* cause of a neurosis.

[5]The book bears the date of 1900 on the title page and this date is usually given as the date of publication.

detailed the mental stratagems that translate their causes into the strange drama the awakening dreamer remembers, and, in the difficult seventh chapter, outlined a comprehensive theory of mind. Its first reception was cool. During six years, only 351 copies were sold; a second edition did not appear until 1909. However, Freud's popularly written *Psychopathology of Everyday Life* of 1901 found a wider audience. Its collection of appealing slips of all sorts made Freud's fundamental point that the mind, however disheveled it might appear, is governed by firm rules. Thus—to give but one typical instance—the presiding officer of the Austrian parliament, facing a disagreeable season, opened it with the formal declaration that it was hereby closed. That "accident" had been prompted by his hidden repugnance for the sessions ahead.

Gradually, though still considered a radical, Freud acquired prestige and supporters. He had quarreled with Fliess in 1900, and, though their correspondence lingered on for some time, the two men never met again. Yet in 1902, after unconscionable delays, apparently generated by anti-Semitism combined with distrust of the maverick innovator, he was finally appointed an associate professor at the University of Vienna. Late that year, Freud and four other Viennese physicians began meeting every Wednesday night in his apartment at Berggasse 19 to discuss psychoanalytic questions; four years after, the group, grown to over a dozen regular participants, employed a paid secretary (Otto Rank) to take minutes and keep records. Finally, in 1908, it was transformed into the Vienna Psychoanalytic Society. At least some medical men (and a few women) were taking Freud's ideas seriously.

In 1905, Freud buttressed the structure of psychoanalytic thought with the second pillar of his theory: the *Three Essays on the Theory of Sexuality*. It outlined perversions and "normal" development from childhood to puberty with a lack of censoriousness and an openness hitherto virtually unknown in medical literature. Again in 1905, Freud brought out his book on jokes and the first of his famous case histories: "Fragment of an Analysis of a Case of Hysteria," nicknamed the "Dora case." He published it to illustrate the uses of dream interpretation in psychoanalysis, and expose his failure to recognize the power of transference in the analytic situation, but its lack of empathy with his embattled teen-age analysand has made it controversial.

In the following decade, Freud enriched the technique of psychoanalysis with three more sophisticated case histories—"Analysis of a Phobia in a Five-Year-Old Boy" ("Little Hans"), "Notes upon a Case of Obsessional Neurosis" ("Rat Man") in 1909, and "Psycho-Analytic Notes on an Autobiographical Account of a Case of Paranoia" ("Schreber Case") in 1911. Despite recent reanalyses, they remain lucid expository models across a wide spectrum of mental ailments. Then, from 1910 on, Freud published pioneering, exceedingly influential papers on technique, to establish psychoanalytic method on sound foundations. Nor did he neglect theory; witness such an important paper as "Formulations on the Two Principles of Mental Functioning" (1911), in which he differentiated between the "primary process," the primitive, unconscious element in the mind, and the "secondary process," largely conscious and controlled.

During these years, Freud also broke out of the circumscribed bounds of clinical and theoretical specialization by publishing papers on religion, literature, sexual mores, biography, sculpture, prehistory, and much else. "Obsessive Actions and Religious Practices" (1907), "Creative Writers and Daydreaming" (1908), " 'Civilized' Sexual Morality and Modern Nervous Illness" (1908), and his widely debated study of the origins of homosexuality, "Leonardo da

Vinci and a Memory of His Childhood" (1910), are only samples of his range. Freud took all of culture as his province. He was realizing the program he had outlined for himself in his youth: to solve some of the great riddles of human existence.

Yet Freud also found the decade from 1905 to 1914 agitating with the progress of, and disagreeable splits within, a rapidly emerging international movement—*his* movement. Psychoanalytic politics took center stage. Two principal sources of hope for the future of Freud's ideas, and later of envenomed contention, were the intelligent, Socialist Viennese physician Alfred Adler (1870–1937), and the original, self-willed Swiss psychiatrist Carl G. Jung (1875–1961). Adler had been among Freud's earliest adherents and remained for some years his most prominent Viennese advocate. But as professional interest in psychoanalysis—not all of it benevolent—grew apace, as Freud's upsetting ideas were being explored at psychiatrists' congresses, Freud aspired to enlarge the reach of psychoanalysis beyond its place of origin. Vienna, with its handful of followers, struck him as provincial, unsuitable as headquarters.

The first breakthrough came in 1906, when Jung, then principal psychiatrist at the renowned clinic Burghölzli in Zurich, sent Freud an offprint. Freud responded promptly; a cordial correspondence blossomed, and the friendship was cemented by Jung's visit to Freud in early 1907. Freud was only fifty, vigorous and productive, but he had long brooded on himself as aging and decrepit. He was seeking a successor who would carry the psychoanalytic dispensation to later generations and into a world larger than the Viennese, Jewish ambiance to which psychoanalysis was then confined. Jung, a formidable presence and energetic debater, was an inspired discovery: he was not old, he was not Viennese, he was not Jewish. Jung was prominent in the first international congress of psychoanalysts at Salzburg in the spring of 1908, and was appointed, the following year, editor of a newly founded *Yearbook*. Freud, delighted with Jung, anointed him his son, his crown prince—accolades that Jung welcomed, indeed encouraged. Hence, when the International Psychoanalytic Association was founded in March 1910, in Nürnberg, Jung was Freud's logical, inevitable, choice for president. Freud's Viennese adherents saw their city displaced by Zurich as the center of psychoanalysis, and did not like it. A compromise was hammered out, and for some time peace reigned in the Vienna Psychoanalytic Society. But Adler was developing distinctive psychological ideas, which featured aggressiveness over sexuality, and "organ inferiority" as a dominant cause of neuroses. A split became inevitable, and, in the summer of 1911, Adler and some of his adherents resigned, leaving Freud and the Freudians in control of the Vienna society.

Freud was not without accolades. In September 1909, he had received an honorary doctorate at Clark University in Worcester, Massachusetts, as had Jung. But like Adler, Jung increasingly diverged from Freud's ideas. He had never been easy with the prominence Freud assigned to the sexual drive—libido. By early 1912, these reservations took a personal turn. In response, Ernest Jones, Freud's principal English lieutenant, formed a defensive secret band of likeminded analysts, the Committee. It consisted of himself, Freud, Sandor Ferenczi (a brilliant adherent from Budapest), the witty Viennese lawyer Hanns Sachs, the astute Berlin clinician and theorist Karl Abraham, and Freud's amanuensis, the autodidact Otto Rank. It seemed needed: by late 1912, the correspondence between Jung and Freud had grown acrimonious and in January 1914, Freud terminated his friendship with Jung. A split was only a matter of time; in the spring of 1914, Jung resigned from his powerful positions in the psychoanalytic movement.

The strains of psychoanalytic politics did not keep Freud from continuing his explorations of an impressive variety of topics. In 1913, he published an audacious, highly speculative venture into psychoanalytic prehistory, *Totem and Taboo,* which specified the moment that savages, in some dim, remote past, entered culture by murdering their father and acquiring guilt feelings. Then, in 1914, he published (anonymously) "The Moses of Michelangelo," uniting his admiration for Michelangelo's brooding sculpture with his powers of observation. In the same year, with an unsettling paper on narcissism, he subverted crucial aspects of psychoanalytic thought by throwing doubts upon his theory of drives—hitherto divided into erotic and egoistic.

But harrowing events on the world stage shouldered aside Freud's reassessment of psychoanalytic theory. On June 28, 1914, Austria's Archduke Francis Ferdinand and his consort were assassinated. Six weeks later, on August 4, Europe was at war. The first casualty for psychoanalysis was Freud's eventually best-known case history, "From the History of an Infantile Neurosis" ("Wolf Man"), written in the fall of 1914, but not published until 1918. Psychoanalytic activity almost ground to a halt. Many potential patients were at the front; most psychoanalysts were drafted into the medical corps; communications between "enemies" like Ernest Jones and Freud were severely truncated; psychoanalytic publications almost vanished; and congresses, the lifeblood of communication, were out of the question. For Freud, these were anxious times in other ways: all three of his sons were in the army, two of them almost daily in mortal danger.

Yet the war did not idle Freud's mind. Having too much time on his hands, he used it to good purpose. Work was a defense against brooding. Between March and July 1915, he wrote a dozen fundamental papers on metapsychology—on the unconscious, on repression, on melancholia; but he refused to gather them into the basic textbook he had planned. He published five of the papers between 1915 and 1917, and destroyed the rest. His enigmatic dissatisfaction with them hints at the discontent that had fueled his paper on narcissism. His map of the mind was inadequate to the evidence he had accumulated in his clinical experience. But he still lacked a satisfactory alternative. That would have to wait until after the war.

Another wartime activity, though more successful, gave Freud only modest pleasure: beginning in 1915, he delivered lectures at the university, published as a single volume in 1917 as *Introductory Lectures on Psycho-Analysis*. With the cunning of the born popularizer, Freud opened with a series on ordinary experiences, slips of the tongue, "unmotivated" forgetting, then turned to dreams and concluded with the technical topic, neuroses. Frequently reprinted and widely translated, these *Introductory Lectures* finally secured Freud a wide audience.

The war dragged on. Originally, somewhat to his surprise, an Austrian patriot, Freud wearied of the endless slaughter. He grew appalled at the chauvinism of intellectuals, the callousness of commanders, the stupidity of politicians. He had not yet fully acknowledged the theoretical significance of aggression, even though psychoanalysts had regularly encountered aggressiveness among their patients. But the war, beastly as it was, confirmed the skeptical psychoanalytic appraisal of human nature.

Signs of revived activity came shortly before the end of hostilities. In September 1918, for the first time since 1913, psychoanalysts from Germany and Austria-Hungary met in Budapest. Two months later, the war was over. To the family's immense relief, all of Freud's sons survived it. But the time for worry was far from over. The defeated powers were faced with revolution, drastically transformed from empires into republics, and saddled with stringent, vindictive peace treaties stripping them of territory and resources. Vienna was hungry, cold, desperate; food and fuel shortages produced deadly ailments—tuberculosis and influenza. In this stressful situation, Freud, who wasted no tears on the departed Hapsburg Empire, proved an energetic, imaginative manager. The portrait of Martha Freud shielding Herr Professor from domestic realities needs revision. Freud dispatched precise requests abroad to relatives, friends, associates, specifying what nourishment and clothing his family needed most, and how to send packages safely. Then, in January 1920, postwar misery struck home with deadly force: Freud's beloved second daughter Sophie, married and living in Hamburg, mother of two children, died in the influenza epidemic.

It has been plausibly argued that her death suggested the pessimistic drive theory that Freud now developed. Actually, he had virtually completed *Beyond the Pleasure Principle* (1920), which first announced Freud's theory of the death drive, the year before. Once Freud had adopted this construct, in which the forces of life, Eros, dramatically confront the forces of death, Thanatos, he found himself unable to think any other way. In 1923, in his classic study *The Ego and the Id,* he completed his revisions. He now proposed a "structural theory" of the mind, which visualizes the mind as divided into three distinct yet interacting agencies: the id (the wholly unconscious domain of the mind, consisting of the drives and of material later repressed), the ego (which is partly conscious and contains the defense mechanisms and the capacities to calculate, reason, and plan), and the super-ego (also only partly conscious, which harbors the conscience and, beyond that, unconscious feelings of guilt). This new scheme did not lead Freud to abandon his classic characterization of mental activity—emphasizing the distance of thoughts from awareness—as either conscious, or preconscious, or wholly unconscious. But he now made the decisive point that many of the mental operations of the ego, and of the super-ego as well, are inaccessible to direct introspection.

Meanwhile, the psychoanalytic movement was flourishing. Freud was becoming a household word, though he detested the sensationalized attention the popular press gave him. Better: in 1920, at the first postwar congress at The Hague, former "enemies" met as friends. Freud was accompanied by his daughter Anna, whom he was then analyzing and who joined the Vienna Psychoanalytic Society in 1922. In that year, the analysts convened in Berlin. It was the last congress Freud ever attended. In April 1923, he was operated on for a growth in his palate. While for months his doctors and closest associates pretended that the growth was benign, by September the truth was out: he had cancer. Severe operations followed in the fall. From then on Freud, compelled to wear a prosthesis, was rarely free of discomfort or pain.

But he never stopped working. While he had trouble speaking, he continued to analyze patients, many of them American physicians who came to Vienna as his "pupils" and returned to analyze in New York or Chicago. He continued to revise his theories. From the mid-1920s on, he wrote controversial papers on female sexuality, and, in 1926, *Inhibitions, Symptoms, and Anxiety,* which reversed his earlier thinking on anxiety, now treating it as a danger signal. Moreover, he wrote essays that found a relatively wide public: *The Future of an Illusion,* a convinced atheist's dissection of religion, in 1927, and, in 1930, *Civilization and Its*

Discontents, a disillusioned look at modern civilization on the verge of catastrophe.

In 1933, that catastrophe came. On January 30, Hitler was appointed chancellor in Germany, and from then on Austrian Nazis, already active, increasingly intervened in politics. The old guard was disappearing: Karl Abraham had died prematurely in 1925; Sandor Ferenczi followed him in 1933. Freud's closest friends were gone. But Freud was unwilling to leave the Vienna he hated and loved: he was too old, he did not want to desert, and besides, the Nazis would never invade his country. On the morning of March 12, 1938, the Germans proved him wrong. As the Nazis marched in, a jubilant populace greeted them. Spontaneous anti-Semitic outrages surpassed anything Germans had witnessed after five years of Nazi rule. Late in March, Anna was summoned to Gestapo headquarters; while she was released unharmed, the trauma changed Freud's mind: he must emigrate. It took months to satisfy the Nazi government's extortions, but on June 4, Freud left for Paris, welcomed by his former analysand and loving disciple, Princess Marie Bonaparte. On June 6, Freud landed in London, preceded by most of his family, "to die in freedom."

Aged and ill, he kept on working. Freud's last completed book, *Moses and Monotheism*, irritated and dismayed his Jewish readers with its assertion that Moses had been an Egyptian: he ended life as he had lived it—a disturber of the peace. He died bravely on September 23, 1939, asking his physician for a lethal dose of morphine. Freud did not believe in personal immortality, but his work lives on.

ABOUT THIS BOOK

Freud's *Interpretation of Dreams*, published in November 1899 (it has become customary to list its date of publication as 1900), was a very substantial and, in parts, for all Freud's literary skills, a very difficult book. It opened with a long chapter reviewing the literature on dreams since antiquity, continued with examples of dream analysis, spent a good deal of space on the techniques of dreams (the so-called "dream work"), and concluded with the notorious seventh chapter in which Freud presented his complex theory of the mind. This was not exactly vacation reading. (In fact, *The Interpretation of Dreams* only sold 351 copies in six years, and a second edition was not called for until 1909.) Aware of this, however reluctant he was to go over the old ground again—he had, after all, worked intensely on *The Interpretation of Dreams* for years—Freud decided that he must offer a popular version of his "dream book," one that would be briefer, freed of the most esoteric theoretical baggage, in short easier to follow. *Über den Traum* was the result. As the book, *On Dreams,* documents, Freud succeeded admirably: the theory of the dream as distorted wish fulfillment is there, as are, in full deployment, the mechanisms of the dream work. Without doubt, Freud was always his own best popularizer.

ON DREAMS

TRANSLATOR'S NOTE

Über den Traum was first published in 1901 as part of a serial publication, *Grenzfragen des Nervenund Seelenlebens,* edited by Löwenfeld and Kurella (Wiesbaden: Bergmann). A second edition was published as a separate brochure by the same firm in 1911; and a third edition in 1921. The work was included in Vol. III of Freud's *Gesammelte Schriften* (Vienna) in 1925 and in Vols. II-III of his *Gesammelte Werke* (London) in 1942. An English translation by M. D. Eder (London: Heinemann) appeared in 1914. A certain amount of fresh material was added in the second German edition, but no substantial changes were made in later issues. The additions are indicated in this entirely new English version.

Almost exactly a year after the publication of *The Interpretation of Dreams*—during the last two or three months of 1900—Freud wrote the present short discussion of the same topic. It offers, of course, a complete contrast to that epoch-making but formidable work. The immense accumulation of detailed observations is represented here by only a few specimens; the elaborate dissection of the theories of earlier writers is entirely absent; and, most important of all, the discussion of the bearing of Freud's study of dreams upon our understanding of the whole structure and functioning of the human mind—a discussion which occupies the last and most difficult chapter of the earlier book—is no more than slightly touched on in these pages. Nevertheless, within the narrow limits which he here imposed on himself, Freud succeeded in giving a comprehensive but easily intelligible account of his views on the nature and mechanism of dreams. Those views, moreover, stand in very little need of correction in the light of Freud's later studies. Indeed, his suggestion in *Beyond the Pleasure Principle* (in 1920) that dreams occurring in traumatic neuroses cannot be regarded as wish fulfillments is perhaps the only major alteration he made in the position sketched out in the following pages.

My grateful thanks are due to Miss Anna Freud for reading my translation through and suggesting a number of changes.

J. S.

I

During the epoch which may be described as prescientific, men had no difficulty in finding an explanation of dreams. When they remembered a dream after waking up, they regarded it as either a favorable or a hostile manifestation by higher powers, demonic and divine. When modes of thought belonging to natural science began to flourish, all this ingenious mythology was transformed into psychology, and today only a small minority of educated people doubt that dreams are a product of the dreamer's own mind.

Since the rejection of the mythological hypothesis, however, dreams have stood in need of explanation. The conditions of their origin, their relation to waking mental life, their dependence upon stimuli which force their way upon perception during the state of sleep, the many peculiarities of their content which are repugnant to waking thought, the inconsistency between their ideational images and the affects attaching to them, and lastly their transitory character, the manner in which waking thought pushes them on one side as something alien to it, and mutilates or extinguishes them in memory—all of these and other problems besides have been awaiting clarification for many hundreds of years, and till now no satisfactory solution of them has been advanced. But what stands in the foreground of our interest is the question of the *significance* of dreams, a question which bears a double sense. It inquires, in the first place, as to the psychical significance of dreaming, as to the relation of dreams to other mental processes, and as to any biological function that they may have; in the second place, it seeks to discover whether dreams can be interpreted, whether the content of individual dreams has a "meaning," such as we are accustomed to find in other psychical structures.

In the assessment of the significance of dreams three lines of thought can be distinguished. One of these, which echoes, as it were, the ancient overvaluation of dreams, is expressed in the writings of certain philosophers. They consider that the basis of dream life is a peculiar state of mental activity, and even go so far as to acclaim that state as an elevation to a higher level. For instance, Schubert [1814] declares that dreams are a liberation of the spirit from the power of external nature, and a freeing of the soul from the bonds of the senses. Other thinkers, without going so far as this, insist nevertheless that dreams arise essentially from mental impulses and represent manifestations of mental forces which have been prevented from expanding freely during the daytime. (Cf. the "dream imagination" of Scherner [1861, 97 f.] and Volkelt [1875, 28 f.].) A large number of observers agree in attributing to dream life a capacity for superior functioning in certain departments at least (*e.g.*, in memory).

In sharp contrast to this, the majority of medical writers adopt a view according to which dreams scarcely reach the level of being psychical phenomena at all. On their theory, the sole instigators of dreams are the sensory and somatic stimuli which either impinge upon the sleeper from outside or become active accidentally in his internal organs. What is dreamed, they contend, has no more claim to sense and meaning than, for instance, the sounds which would be produced if "the ten fingers of a man who knows nothing of music were wandering over the keys of a piano." [Strüm-pell, 1874, 84.] Dreams are described by Binz [1878, 35] as being no more than "somatic processes which are in every case useless and in many cases positively pathological." All the characteristics of dream life would thus be explained as being due to the disconnected activity of separate organs or groups of cells in an otherwise sleeping brain, an activity forced upon them by physiological stimuli.

Popular opinion is but little affected by this scientific judgment and is not concerned as to the sources of dreams; it seems to persist in the belief that nevertheless dreams have a meaning, which relates to the prediction of the future and which can be discovered by some process of interpreta-tion of a content which is often confused and puzzling. The methods of interpretation employed consist in transforming the content of the dream as it is remembered, either by replacing it piecemeal in accordance with a fixed key, or by replacing the dream as a whole by another whole to which it stands in a symbolic relation. Serious-minded people smile at these efforts: *Träume sind Schäume*—"dreams are froth."

II

_____

One day I discovered to my great astonishment that the
view of dreams which came nearest to the truth was not the
medical but the popular one, half-involved though it still was
in superstition. For I had been led to fresh conclusions on
the subject of dreams by applying to them a new method of
psychological investigation which had done excellent service
in the solution of phobias, obsessions and delusions, etc.
Since then, under the name of "psychoanalysis," it has
found acceptance by a whole school of research workers.
The numerous analogies that exist between dream life and
a great variety of conditions of psychical illness in waking life
have indeed been correctly observed by many medical inves-
tigators. There seemed, therefore, good ground for hoping
that a method of investigation which had given satisfactory
results in the case of psychopathic structures would also be
of use in throwing light upon dreams. Phobias and obsessions are as alien to normal consciousness as dreams are to
waking consciousness; their origin is as unknown to consciousness as that of dreams. In the case of these psychopathic structures practical considerations led to an investigation of their origin and mode of development; for experience
had shown that the discovery of the trains of thought which,

concealed from consciousness, connect the pathological ideas with the remaining contents of the mind is equivalent to a resolution of the symptoms and has as its consequence the mastering of ideas which till then could not be inhibited. Thus psychotherapy was the starting point of the procedure of which I made use for the explanation of dreams.

This procedure is easily described, although instruction and practice would be necessary before it could be put into effect.

If we make use of it on someone else, let us say on a patient with a phobia, we require him to direct his attention on to the idea in question, not, however, to reflect upon it as he has done so often already, but to take notice of *whatever occurs to his mind without any exception* and report it to the physician. If he should then assert that his attention is unable to grasp anything at all, we dismiss this with an energetic assurance that a complete absence of any ideational subject matter is quite impossible. And in fact very soon numerous ideas will occur to him and will lead on to others; but they will invariably be prefaced by a judgment on the part of the self-observer to the effect that they are senseless or unimportant, that they are irrelevant, and that they occurred to him by chance and without any connection with the topic under consideration. We perceive at once that it was this critical attitude which prevented the subject from reporting any of these ideas, and which indeed had previously prevented them from becoming conscious. If we can induce him to abandon his criticism of the ideas that occur to him, and to continue pursuing the trains of thought which will emerge so long as he keeps his attention turned upon them, we find ourselves in possession of a quantity of psychical material, which we soon find is clearly connected with the pathological idea which was our starting point; this material will soon reveal connections between the pathological idea and other ideas, and will eventually enable us to replace the pathological idea by a new one which fits into the nexus of thought in an intelligible fashion.

This is not the place in which to give a detailed account of the premises upon which this experiment was based, or the consequences which follow from its invariable success. It will therefore be enough to say that we obtain material that enables us to resolve any pathological idea if we turn our attention precisely to those associations which are "involuntary," which "interfere with our reflection," and which are normally dismissed by our critical faculty as worthless rubbish.

If we make use of this procedure upon *ourselves,* we can best assist the investigation by at once writing down what are at first unintelligible associations.

I will now show what results follow if I apply this method of investigation to dreams. Any example of a dream should in fact be equally appropriate for the purpose; but for particular reasons I will choose some dream of my own, one which seems obscure and meaningless as I remember it, and one which has the advantage of brevity. A dream which I actually had last night will perhaps meet these requirements. Its content, as I noted it down immediately after waking up, was as follows:

> "Company at table or table d'hôte . . . spinach was being eaten . . . Frau E. L. was sitting beside me; she was turning her whole attention to me and laid her hand on my knee in an intimate manner. I removed her hand unresponsively. She then said: 'But you've always had such beautiful eyes.' . . . I then had an indistinct picture of two eyes, as though it were a drawing or like the outline of a pair of spectacles. . . ."

This was the whole of the dream, or at least all that I could remember of it. It seemed to me obscure and meaningless, but above all surprising. Frau E. L. is a person with whom I have hardly at any time been on friendly terms, nor, so far as I know, have I ever wished to have any closer relations with her. I have not seen her for a long time, and her name has not, I believe, been mentioned during the last few days. The dream process was not accompanied by affects of any kind.

Reflecting over this dream brought me no nearer to understanding it. I determined, however, to set down without any premeditation or criticism the associations which presented themselves to my self-observation. As I have found, it is advisable for this purpose to divide a dream into its elements and to find the associations attaching to each of these fragments separately.

Company at table or table d'hôte—this at once reminded me of an episode which occurred late yesterday evening. I came away from a small party in the company of a friend who offered to take a cab and drive me home in it. "I prefer taking a cab with a taximeter," he said. "It occupies one's mind so agreeably; one always has something to look at." When we had taken our places in the cab and the driver had set the dial, so that the first charge of 60 hellers [=6d.] became visible, I carried the joke further. "We've only just got in," I said, "and already we owe him 60 hellers. A cab with a taximeter always reminds me of a table d'hôte. It makes me avaricious and selfish, because it keeps on reminding me of what I owe. My debt seems to be growing too fast, and I'm afraid of getting the worst of the bargain; and in just the same way at a table d'hôte I can't avoid feeling in a comic way that I'm getting too little, and must keep an eye on my own interests." I went on to quote, somewhat discursively:

Ihr führt ins Leben uns hinein,
Ihr lasst den Armen schuldig werden. [1]

And now a second association to "table d'hôte." A few weeks ago, while we were at table in a hotel at a mountain resort in the Tyrol, I was very much annoyed because I thought my wife was not being sufficiently reserved toward some people sitting near us whose acquaintance I had no desire at all to make. I asked her to concern herself more with me than with these strangers. This was again *as though I were getting the worst of the bargain at the table d'hôte.* I was struck too by the contrast between my wife's behavior at table and that of Frau E. L. in the dream, who "turned her whole attention to me."

To proceed, I now saw that the events in the dream were a reproduction of a small episode of a precisely similar kind which occurred between my wife and me at the time at which I was secretly courting her. The caress which she gave me under the tablecloth was her reply to a pressing love letter. In the dream, however, my wife was replaced by a comparative stranger—E. L.

Frau E. L. is the daughter of a man to whom I was once *in debt.* I could not help noticing that this revealed an unsuspected connection between parts of the content of the dream and my associations. If one follows the train of association starting out from one element of a dream's content,

---

[1][These lines are from one of the Harp-player's songs in Goethe's *Wilhelm Meister.* In the original the words are addressed to the Heavenly Powers and may be translated literally: "You lead us into life, you make the poor creature guilty." But the words *Armen* and *schuldig* are both capable of bearing another meaning. *Armen* might mean "poor" in the financial sense and *schuldig* might mean "in debt." So in the present context the last line could be rendered: "You make the poor man fall into debt."]

one is soon brought back to another of its elements. My associations to the dream were bringing to light connections which were not visible in the dream itself.

If a person expects one to keep an eye on his interests without any advantage to oneself, his artlessness is apt to provoke the scornful question: "Do you suppose I'm going to do this or that for the sake of your *beaux yeux* [beautiful eyes]?" That being so, Frau E. L.'s speech in the dream, "You've always had such beautiful eyes," can only have meant: "People have always done everything for you for love; you have always had everything *without paying for it.*" The truth is, of course, just the contrary: I have always paid dearly for whatever advantage I have had from other people. The fact that my friend took me home yesterday in a cab *without my paying for it* must, after all, have made an impression on me.

Incidentally, the friend whose guests we were yesterday has often put me in his debt. Only recently I allowed an opportunity of repaying him to slip by. He has had only one present from me—an antique bowl, around which there are *eyes* painted: what is known as an *"occhiale,"* to avert the *evil eye.* Moreover he is an *eye surgeon.* The same evening I asked him about a woman patient, whom I had sent on to him for a consultation to fit her with *spectacles.*

As I now perceived, almost all the elements of the dream's content had been brought into the new context. For the sake of consistency, however, the further question might be asked of why *spinach,* of all things, was being served in the dream. The answer was that *spinach* reminded me of an episode which occurred not long ago at our family table, when one of the children—and precisely the one who really deserves to be admired for his *beautiful eyes*—refused to eat any spinach. I myself behaved in just the same way when I was a child; for a long time I detested spinach, till eventually my taste changed and promoted that vegetable into one of my favorite foods. My own early life and my child's were thus brought together by the mention of this dish. "You ought to be glad to have spinach," the little gourmet's mother exclaimed; "there are children who would be only too pleased to have spinach." Thus I was reminded of the duties of parents to their children. Goethe's words

Ihr führt ins Leben uns hinein,
Ihr lasst den Armen schuldig werden

gained a fresh meaning in this connection.[2]

I will pause here to survey the results I had so far reached in my dream analysis. By following the associations which arose from the separate elements of the dream divorced from their context, I arrived at a number of thoughts and recollections, which I could not fail to recognize as important products of my mental life. This material revealed by the analysis of the dream was intimately connected with the dream's content, yet the connection was of such a kind that I could never have inferred the fresh material from that content. The dream was unemotional, disconnected and unintelligible; but while I was producing the thoughts behind the dream, I was aware of intense and well-founded affective impulses; the thoughts themselves fell at once into logical chains, in which certain central ideas made their appearance more than once. Thus, the contrast between "selfish" and "unselfish," and the elements "being in debt" and "without paying for it" were central ideas of this kind,

---

[2][See footnote 1. The first line of the couplet might now be taken to mean that the verses are addressed to parents.]

not represented in the dream itself. I could draw closer together the threads in the material revealed by the analysis, and I could then show that they converge upon a single nodal point, but considerations of a personal and not of a scientific nature prevent my doing so in public. I should be obliged to betray many things which had better remain my secret, for on my way to discovering the solution of the dream all kinds of things were revealed which I was unwilling to admit even to myself. Why then, it will be asked, have I not chosen some other dream, whose analysis is better suited for reporting, so that I could produce more convincing evidence of the meaning and connectedness of the material uncovered by analysis? The answer is that *every* dream with which I might try to deal would lead to things equally hard to report and would impose an equal discretion upon me. Nor should I avoid this difficulty by bringing up someone else's dream for analysis, unless circumstances enabled me to drop all disguise without damage to the person who had confided in me.

At the point which I have now reached, I am led to regard the dream as a sort of *substitute* for the thought processes, full of meaning and emotion, at which I arrived after the completion of the analysis. We do not yet know the nature of the process which has caused the dream to be generated from these thoughts, but we can see that it is wrong to regard it as purely physical and without psychical meaning, as a process which has arisen from the isolated activity of separate groups of brain cells aroused from sleep.

Two other things are already clear. The content of the dream is very much shorter than the thoughts of which I regard it as a substitute; and analysis has revealed that the instigator of the dream was an unimportant event of the evening before I dreamed it.

I should, of course, not draw such far-reaching conclusions if only a single dream analysis was at my disposal. If experience shows me, however, that by uncritically pursuing the associations arising from *any* dream I can arrive at a similar train of thoughts, among the elements of which the constituents of the dream reappear and which are interconnected in a rational and intelligible manner, then it will be safe to disregard the slight possibility that the connections observed in a first experiment might be due to chance. I think I am justified, therefore, in adopting a terminology which will crystallize our new discovery. In order to contrast the dream as it is retained in my memory with the relevant material discovered by analyzing it, I shall speak of the former as the *"manifest* content of the dream" and the latter—without, in the first instance, making any further distinction—as the *"latent* content of the dream." I am now faced by two new problems which have not hitherto been formulated. (1) What is the psychical process which has transformed the latent content of the dream into the manifest one which is known to me from my memory? (2) What are the motive or motives which have necessitated this transformation? I shall describe the process which transforms the latent into the manifest content of dreams as the "dream work." The counterpart to this activity—one which brings about a transformation in the opposite direction—is already known to us as the work of analysis. The remaining problems arising out of dreams—questions as to the instigators of dreams, as to the origin of their material, as to their possible meaning, as to the possible function of dreaming, and as to the reasons for dreams being forgotten—all these problems will be discussed by me on the basis, not of the manifest, but of the newly discovered latent dream content. Since I attribute all the contradictory and incorrect views upon dream life which appear in the literature of the subject to ignorance of the latent content of dreams as revealed by analysis, I shall be at the greatest pains henceforward to avoid confusing the *manifest dream* with the *latent dream thoughts.*

III

The transformation of the latent dream thoughts into the manifest dream content deserves all our attention, since it is the first instance known to us of psychical material being changed over from one mode of expression to another, from a mode of expression which is immediately intelligible to us to another which we can only come to understand with the help of guidance and effort, though it, too, must be recognized as a function of our mental activity.

Dreams can be divided into three categories in respect of the relation between their latent and manifest content. In the first place, we may distinguish those dreams which *make sense* and are at the same time *intelligible*, which, that is to say, can be inserted without further difficulty into the context of our mental life. We have numbers of such dreams. They are for the most part short and appear to us in general to deserve little attention, since there is nothing astonishing or strange about them. Incidentally, their occurrence constitutes a powerful argument against the theory according to which dreams originate from the isolated activity of separate groups of brain cells. They give no indication of reduced or fragmentary psychical activity, but nevertheless we never question the fact of their being dreams, and do not confuse them with the products of waking life. A second group is formed by those dreams which, though they are connected in themselves and have a clear sense, nevertheless have a *bewildering* effect, because we cannot see how to fit that sense into our mental life. Such would be the case if we were to dream, for instance, that a relative of whom we were fond had died of the plague, when we had no reason for expecting, fearing or assuming any such thing; we should ask in astonishment: "How did I get hold of such an idea?" The third group, finally, contains those dreams which are without either sense or intelligibility, which seem *disconnected, confused,* and *meaningless.* The preponderating majority of the products of our dreaming exhibit these characteristics, which are the basis of the low opinion in which dreams are held and of the medical theory that they are the outcome of a restricted mental activity. The most evident signs of incoherence are seldom absent, especially in dream compositions of any considerable length and complexity.

The contrast between the manifest and latent content of dreams is clearly of significance only for dreams of the second and more particularly of the third category. It is there that we are faced by riddles which only disappear after we have replaced the manifest dream by the latent thoughts behind it; and it was on a specimen of the last category—a confused and unintelligible dream—that the analysis which I have just recorded was carried out. Contrary to our expectation, however, we came up against motives which prevented us from becoming fully acquainted with the latent dream thoughts. A repetition of similar experiences may lead us to suspect that there is an intimate and regular relation between the unintelligible and confused nature of dreams and the difficulty of reporting the thoughts behind them.[1] Before inquiring into the nature of this relation, we

---

[1] [The last clause is in spaced type in the original.]

may with advantage turn our attention to the more easily intelligible dreams of the first category, in which the manifest and the latent content coincide, and there appears to be a consequent saving in dream work.

Moreover, an examination of these dreams offers advantages from another standpoint. For *children's* dreams are of that kind—significant and not puzzling. Here, incidentally, we have a further argument against tracing the origin of dreams to dissociated cerebral activity during sleep. For why should a reduction in psychical functioning of this kind be a characteristic of the state of sleep in the case of adults but not in that of children? On the other hand, we shall be fully justified in expecting that an explanation of psychical processes in children, in whom they may well be greatly simplified, may turn out to be an indispensable prelude to the investigation of the psychology of adults.

I will therefore record a few instances of dreams which I have collected from children. A little girl nineteen months old had been kept without food all day because she had had an attack of vomiting in the morning; her nurse declared that she had been upset by eating strawberries. During the night after this day of starvation she was heard saying her own name in her sleep and adding: *"Stwawbewwies, wild stwawbewwies, omblet, pap!"* She was thus dreaming of eating a meal, and she laid special stress in her menu on the particular delicacy of which, as she had reason to expect, she would only be allowed scanty quantities in the near future. A little boy of twenty-two months had a similar dream of a feast which he had been denied. The day before, he had been obliged to present his uncle with a gift of a basket of fresh cherries, of which he himself, of course, had only been allowed to taste a single sample. He awoke with this cheerful news: *"Hermann eaten all the chewwies!"* One day a girl of three and a quarter made a trip across a lake. The voyage was evidently not long enough for her, for she cried when she had to get off the boat. Next morning she reported that during the night she had been for a trip on the lake: she had been continuing her interrupted voyage. A boy of five and a quarter showed signs of dissatisfaction in the course of a walk in the neighborhood of the Dachstein.[2] Each time a new mountain came into view he asked if it was the Dachstein and finally refused to visit a waterfall with the rest of the company. His behavior was attributed to fatigue; but it found a better explanation when next morning he reported that he had dreamed that *he had climbed up the Dachstein.* He had evidently had the idea that the expedition would end in a climb up the Dachstein, and had become depressed when the promised mountain never came in view. He made up in his dream for what the previous day had failed to give him. An eight-year-old girl had an exactly similar dream. In the course of a walk her father had stopped short of their intended goal as the hour was getting late. On their way back she had noticed a signpost bearing the name of another landmark; and her father had promised to take her there as well another time. Next morning she met her father with the news that she had dreamed that *he had been with her to both places.*

The common element in all these children's dreams is obvious. All of them fulfilled wishes which were active during the day but had remained unfulfilled. The dreams were simple and undisguised *wish fulfillments.*

Here is another child's dream, which, though at first sight it is not quite easy to understand, is also nothing more than a wish fulfillment. A little girl not quite four years old had been brought to town from the country because she was suffering from an attack of poliomyelitis. She spent the

---

[2][A mountain in the Austrian Alps.]

night with an aunt who had no children, and was put to sleep in a large bed—much too large for her, of course. Next morning she said she had had a dream that *the bed had been far too small for her, and that there had been no room for her in it.* It is easy to recognize this dream as a wishful dream if we remember that children very often express a wish *"to be big."* The size of the bed was a disagreeable reminder of her smallness to the would-be big child; she therefore corrected the unwelcome relation in her dream, and grew so big that even the large bed was too small for her.

Even when the content of children's dreams becomes complicated and subtle, there is never any difficulty in recognizing them as wish fulfillments. An eight-year-old boy had a dream that he was driving in a chariot with Achilles and that Diomed was the charioteer. It was shown that the day before he had been deep in a book of legends about the Greek heroes; and it was easy to see that he had taken the heroes as his models and was sorry not to be living in their days.[3]

This small collection throws a direct light on a further characteristic of children's dreams: their connection with daytime life. The wishes which are fulfilled in them are carried over from daytime and as a rule from the day before, and in waking life they have been accompanied by intense emotion. Nothing unimportant or indifferent, or nothing which would strike a child as such, finds its way into the content of their dreams.

Numerous examples of dreams of this infantile type can be found occurring in adults as well, though, as I have said, they are usually brief in content. Thus a number of people

---

[3] [Most of these children's dreams will be found reported in greater detail in *The Interpretation of Dreams* (1900), Chapter III, and in the eighth of Freud's *Introductory Lectures* (1916–17).]

regularly respond to a stimulus of thirst during the night with dreams of drinking, which thus endeavor to get rid of the stimulus and enable sleep to continue. In some people "dreams of convenience" of this kind often occur before waking, when the necessity for getting up presents itself. They dream that they are already up and at the washstand, or that they are already at the school or office where they are due at some particular time. During the night before a journey we not infrequently dream of having arrived at our destination; so too, before a visit to the theater or a party, a dream will often anticipate the pleasure that lies ahead—out of impatience, as it were. In other dreams the wish fulfillment is expressed a stage more indirectly: some connection or implication must be established—that is, the work of interpretation must be started—before the wish fulfillment can be recognized. A man told me, for instance, that his young wife had had a dream that her period had started. I reflected that if this young woman had missed her period she must have known that she was faced with a pregnancy. Thus when she reported her dream she was announcing her pregnancy, and the meaning of the dream was to represent as fulfilled her wish that the pregnancy might be postponed for a while. Under unusual or extreme conditions dreams of this infantile character are particularly common. Thus the leader of a polar expedition has recorded that the members of his expedition, while they were wintering in the ice field and living on a monotonous diet and short rations, regularly dreamed, like children, of large meals, of mountains of tobacco, and of being back home.[4]

It by no means rarely happens that in the course of a comparatively long, complicated and, on the whole, confused dream one particularly clear portion stands out, which

---

[4][Quoted in full in *The Interpretation of Dreams* (1900), Chapter III.]

contains an unmistakable wish fulfillment, but which is
bound up with some other, unintelligible material. But in
the case of adults, anyone with some experience in analyzing
their dreams will find to his surprise that even those dreams
which have an appearance of being transparently clear[5] are
seldom as simple as those of children, and that behind the
obvious wish fulfillment some other meaning may lie concealed.

It would indeed be a simple and satisfactory solution of
the riddle of dreams if the work of analysis were to enable
us to trace even the meaningless and confused dreams of
adults back to the infantile type of fulfillment of an intensely
felt wish of the previous day. There can be no doubt, however, that appearances do not speak in favor of such an
expectation. Dreams are usually full of the most indifferent
and strangest material, and there is no sign in their content
of the fulfillment of any wish.

But before taking leave of infantile dreams with their
undisguised wish fulfillments, I must not omit to mention
one principal feature of dreams, which has long been evident and which emerges particularly clearly precisely in this
group. Every one of these dreams can be replaced by an
optative clause: "Oh, if only the trip on the lake had lasted
longer!"—"If only I were already washed and dressed!"—
"If only I could have kept the cherries instead of giving
them to Uncle!" But dreams give us more than such optative clauses. They show us the wish as already fulfilled; they
represent its fulfillment as real and present; and the material
employed in dream representation consists principally,
though not exclusively, of situations and of sensory images,
mostly of a visual character. Thus, even in this infantile

---

[5] [*"Durchsichtigen"* in the first edition. In the second and subsequent
editions misprinted *"undurchsichtigen."*]

group, a species of transformation, which deserves to be described as dream work, is not completely absent: a thought expressed in the optative has been replaced by a representation in the present tense.[6]

---

[6][The last clause is in spaced type in the original.]

IV

We shall be inclined to suppose that a transformation of some such kind has occurred even in confused dreams, though we cannot tell whether what has been transformed was an optative in their case too. There are, however, two passages in the specimen dream which I have reported, and with whose analysis we have made some headway, that give us reason to suspect something of the kind. The analysis showed that my wife had concerned herself with some other people at table, and that I had found this disagreeable; the dream contained precisely the opposite of this—the person who took the place of my wife was turning her whole attention to me. But a disagreeable experience can give rise to no more suitable wish than that its opposite might have occurred—which was what the dream represented as fulfilled. There was an exactly similar relation between the bitter thought revealed in the analysis that I had never had anything free of cost and the remark made by the woman in the dream—"You've always had such beautiful eyes." Some part of the opposition between the manifest and the latent content of dreams is thus attributable to wish fulfillment.

But another achievement of the dream work, tending as it does to produce incoherent dreams, is even more striking. If in any particular instance we compare the number of

ideational elements or the space taken up in writing them
down in the case of the dream and of the dream thoughts
to which the analysis leads us and of which traces are to be
found in the dream itself, we shall be left in no doubt that
the dream work has carried out a work of compression or
condensation on a large scale. It is impossible at first to form
any judgment of the degree of this condensation; but the
deeper we plunge into a dream analysis the more impressive
it seems. From every element in a dream's content associative threads branch out in two or more directions; every
situation in a dream seems to be put together out of two or
more impressions or experiences. For instance, I once had
a dream of a sort of swimming pool, in which the bathers
were scattering in all directions; at one point on the edge of
the pool someone was standing and bending toward one of
the people bathing, as though to help her out of the water.
This situation was put together from a memory of an experience I had had at puberty and from two paintings, one of
which I had seen shortly before the dream. One was a
picture from Schwind's series illustrating the legend of
Mélusine, which showed the water nymphs surprised in
their pool (cf the scattering bathers in the dream); the other
was a picture of the Deluge by an Italian Master; while the
little experience remembered from my puberty was of having seen the instructor at a swimming school helping a lady
out of the water who had stopped in until after the time set
aside for men bathers. In the case of the example which I
chose for interpretation, an analysis of the situation led me
to a small series of recollections each of which contributed
something to the content of the dream. In the first place,
there was the episode from the time of my engagement of
which I have already spoken. The pressure upon my hand
under the table, which was a part of that episode, provided
the dream with the detail "under the table"—a detail which

I had to add as an afterthought to my memory of the dream. In the episode itself there was, of course, no question of "turning to me"; the analysis showed that this element was the fulfillment of a wish by presenting the opposite of an actual event, and that it related to my wife's behavior at the table d'hôte. But behind this recent recollection there lay concealed an exactly similar and far more important scene from the time of our engagement, which estranged us for a whole day. The intimate laying of a hand on my knee belonged to a quite different context and was concerned with quite other people. This element in the dream was in turn the starting point of two separate sets of memories—and so on.

The material in the dream thoughts which is packed together for the purpose of constructing a dream situation must, of course, in itself be adaptable for that purpose. There must be one or more *common elements* in all the components. The dream work then proceeds just as Francis Galton did in constructing his family photographs. It superimposes, as it were, the different components upon one another. The common element in them then stands out clearly in the composite picture, while contradictory details more or less wipe one another out. This method of production also explains to some extent the varying degrees of characteristic vagueness shown by so many elements in the content of dreams. Basing itself on this discovery, dream interpretation has laid down the following rule: in analyzing a dream, if an uncertainty can be resolved into an "either—or," we must replace it for purposes of interpretation by an "and," and take each of the apparent alternatives as an independent starting point for a series of associations.

If a common element of this kind between the dream thoughts is not present, the dream work sets about *creating* one, so that it may be possible for the thoughts to be given a common representation in the dream. The most convenient way of bringing together two dream thoughts which, to start with, have nothing in common, is to alter the verbal form of one of them, and thus bring it halfway to meet the other, which may be similarly clothed in a new form of words. A parallel process is involved in hammering out a rhyme, where a similar sound has to be sought for in the same way as a common element is in our present case. A large part of the dream work consists in the creation of intermediate thoughts of this kind which are often highly ingenious, though they frequently appear farfetched; these then form a link between the common representation in the manifest content of the dream and the dream thoughts, which differ from one another both in form and essence and have been determined by the exciting factors of the dream. The analysis of our sample dream affords us an instance of this kind in which a thought has been given a new form in order to bring it into contact with another which is essentially foreign to it. In carrying out the analysis I came upon the following thought: *"I should like to get something sometimes without paying for it."* But in that form the thought could not be employed in the dream content. It was therefore given a fresh form: *"I should like to get some enjoyment without cost ['Kosten ']."*[1] Now the word *Kosten* in its second sense fits into the "table d'hôte" circle of ideas, and could thus be represented in the *"spinach"* which was served in the dream. When a dish appears at our table and the children refuse it, their mother begins by trying persuasion, and urges them *"just to taste ['kosten'] a bit of it."* It may seem strange that the dream work should make such free use of verbal ambiguity, but further experience will teach us that the occurrence is quite a common one.

---

[1][The German word *Kosten* means both "cost" and "to taste."]

The process of condensation further explains certain constituents of the content of dreams which are peculiar to them and are not found in waking ideation. What I have in mind are "collective" and "composite figures" and the strange "composite structures," which are creations not unlike the composite animals invented by the folk-imagination of the Orient. The latter, however, have already assumed stereotyped shapes in our thought, whereas in dreams fresh composite forms are being perpetually constructed in an inexhaustible variety. We are all of us familiar with such structures from our own dreams.

There are many sorts of ways in which figures of this kind can be put together. I may build up a figure by giving it the features of two people; or I may give it the form of one person but think of it in the dream as having the name of another person; or I may have a visual picture of one person, but put it in a situation which is appropriate to another. In all these cases the combination of different persons into a single representative in the content of the dream has a meaning; it is intended to indicate an "and" or "just as," or to compare the original persons with each other in some particular respect, which may even be specified in the dream itself. As a rule, however, this common element between the combined persons can only be discovered by analysis, and is only indicated in the contents of the dream by the formation of the collective figure.

The composite structures which occur in dreams in such immense numbers are put together in an equal variety of ways, and the same rules apply to their resolution. There is no need for me to quote any instances. Their strangeness disappears completely when once we have made up our minds not to class them with the objects of our waking perception, but to remember that they are products of dream condensation and are emphasizing in an effectively

abbreviated form some common characteristic of the objects
which they are thus combining. Here again the common
element has as a rule to be discovered by analysis. The
content of the dream merely says, as it were, "all these
things have an element *x* in common." The dissection of
these composite structures by means of analysis is often the
shortest way to finding the meaning of a dream. Thus, I
dreamed on one occasion that I was sitting on a bench with
one of my former University teachers, and that the bench,
which was surrounded by other benches, was moving forward at a rapid pace. This was a combination of a lecture
theater and a *trottoir roulant.* [2] I will not pursue this train of
ideas further. Another time I was sitting in a railway carriage
and holding on my lap an object in the shape of a top hat
[*"Zylinderhut,"* literally "cylinder hat"], which, however,
was made of transparent glass. The situation made me think
at once of the proverb: *Mit dem Hute in der Hand kommt
man durchs ganze Land.* [3] The glass cylinder led me by a
short detour to think of an incandescent gas mantle; and I
soon saw that I should like to make a discovery which would
make me as rich and independent as my fellow countryman
Dr. Auer von Welsbach was made by his, and that I should
like to travel instead of stopping in Vienna. In the dream
I was traveling with my discovery, the hat in the shape of
a glass cylinder—a discovery which, it is true, was not as yet
of any great practical use. The dream work is particularly
fond of representing two *contrary* ideas by the same composite structure. Thus, for instance, a woman had a dream in
which she saw herself carrying a tall spray of flowers, such
as the angel is represented as holding in pictures of the

---

[2] [The *"trottoir roulant"* was a moving roadway installed at the Paris Exhibi-
tion of 1900.]
[3] ["If you go hat in hand, you can cross the whole land."]

Annunciation. (This stood for innocence; incidentally, her own name was Maria.) On the other hand, the spray was covered with large white[4] flowers like camellias. (This stood for the opposite of innocence; it was associated with *La dame aux camélias.*)

A good proportion of what we have learned about condensation in dreams may be summarized in this formula: each element in the content of a dream is "overdetermined" by material in the dream thoughts; it is not derived from a *single* element in the dream thoughts, but may be traced back to a whole number. These elements need not necessarily be closely related to each other in the dream thoughts themselves; they may belong to the most widely separated regions of the fabric of those thoughts. A dream element is, in the strictest sense of the word, the "representative" of all this disparate material in the content of the dream. But analysis reveals yet another side of the complicated relation between the content of the dream and the dream thoughts. Just as connections lead from each element of the dream to several dream thoughts, so as a rule a single dream thought is represented by more than one dream element; the threads of association do not simply converge from the dream thoughts to the dream content, they cross and interweave with each other many times over in the course of their journey.

Condensation, together with the transformation of thoughts into situations ("dramatization"), is the most important and peculiar characteristic of the dream work. So far, however, nothing has transpired as to any *motive* necessitating this compression of the material.

---

[4][This should probably be "red." The flowers are so described in the much fuller account of the dream given in *The Interpretation of Dreams* (1900) at the end of Section D of Chapter VI.]

V

In the case of the complicated and confused dreams with which we are now concerned, condensation and dramatization alone are not enough to account for the whole of the impression that we gain of the dissimilarity between the content of the dream and the dream thoughts. We have evidence of the operation of a third factor, and this evidence deserves careful sifting.

. First and foremost, when by means of analysis, we have arrived at a knowledge of the dream thoughts, we observe that the manifest dream content deals with quite different material from the latent thoughts. This, to be sure, is no more than an appearance, which evaporates under closer examination, for we find ultimately that the whole of the dream content is derived from the dream thoughts, and that almost all the dream thoughts are represented in the dream content. Nevertheless, something of the distinction still remains. What stands out boldly and clearly in the dream as its essential content must, after analysis, be satisfied with playing an extremely subordinate rôle among the dream thoughts; and what, on the evidence of our feelings, can claim to be the most prominent among the dream thoughts is either not present at all as ideational material in the content of the dream or is only remotely alluded to in some obscure region of it. We may put it in this way: in the course of the dream work the psychical intensity passes over from the thoughts and ideas to which it properly belongs on to others which in our judgment have no claim to any such emphasis.[1] No other process contributes so much to concealing the meaning of a dream and to making the connection between the dream content and the dream thoughts unrecognizable. In the course of this process, which I shall describe as "dream displacement," the psychical intensity, significance or affective potentiality of the thoughts is, as we further find, transformed into sensory vividness. We assume as a matter of course that the most distinct element in the manifest content of a dream is the most important one; but in fact [owing to the displacement that has occurred] it is often an *indistinct* element which turns out to be the most direct derivative of the essential dream thought.

What I have called dream displacement might equally be described [in Nietzsche's phrase] as "a transvaluation of psychical values." I shall not have given an exhaustive estimate of this phenomenon, however, unless I add that this work of displacement or transvaluation is performed to a very varying degree in different dreams. There are dreams which come about almost without any displacement. These are the ones which make sense and are intelligible, such, for instance, as those which we have recognized as undisguised wishful dreams. On the other hand, there are dreams in which not a single piece of the dream thoughts has retained its own psychical value, or in which everything that is essential in the dream thoughts has been replaced by something trivial. And we can find a complete series of transitional cases between these two extremes. The more obscure and confused a dream appears to be, the greater the share in its

---

[1] [This clause is in spaced type in the original.]

construction which may be attributed to the factor of displacement.

Our specimen dream exhibits displacement to this extent at least, that its content seems to have a different *center* from its dream thoughts. In the foreground of the dream content a prominent place is taken by a situation in which a woman seems to be making advances to me; while in the dream thoughts the chief emphasis is laid on a wish for once to enjoy unselfish love, love which "costs nothing"—an idea concealed behind the phrase about "beautiful eyes" and the far-fetched allusion to "spinach."

If we undo dream displacement by means of analysis, we obtain what seems to be completely trustworthy information on two much-disputed problems concerning dreams: as to their instigators and as to their connection with waking life. There are dreams which immediately reveal their derivation from events of the day; there are others in which no trace of any such derivation is to be discovered. If we seek the help of analysis, we find that every dream without any possible exception goes back to an impression of the past few days, or, it is probably more correct to say, of the day immediately preceding the dream, of the "dream day." The impression which plays the part of dream instigator may be such an important one that we feel no surprise at being concerned with it in the daytime, and in that case we rightly speak of the dream as carrying on with the significant interests of our waking life. As a rule, however, if a connection is to be found in the content of the dream with any impression of the previous day, that impression is so trivial, insignificant and unmemorable, that it is only with difficulty that we ourselves can recall it. And in such cases, the content of the dream itself, even if it is connected and intelligible, seems to be concerned with the most indifferent trivialities, which would be unworthy of our interest if we were awake. A good

deal of the contempt in which dreams are held is due to the
preference thus shown in their content for what is indifferent and trivial.

Analysis does away with the misleading appearance upon
which this derogatory judgment is founded. If the content
of a dream puts forward some indifferent impression as
being its instigator, analysis invariably brings to light a significant experience, and one by which the dreamer has good
reason to be stirred. This experience has been replaced by
the indifferent one, with which it is connected by copious
associative links. Where the content of the dream treats of
insignificant and uninteresting ideational material, analysis
uncovers the numerous associative paths connecting these
trivialities with things that are of the highest psychical im-
portance in the dreamer's estimation. If what make their
way into the content of dreams are impressions and material
which are indifferent and trivial rather than justifiably stirring and interesting, that is only the effect of the process
of displacement.[2] If we answer our questions about dream
instigators and the connection between dreaming and daily
affairs on the basis of the new insight we have gained from
replacing the manifest by the latent content of dreams, we
arrive at these conclusions: dreams are never concerned with
things with which we should not think it worth while to
be concerned during the day, and trivialities which do not
affect us during the day are unable to pursue us in our
sleep.[3]

What was the dream instigator in the specimen that we
have chosen for analysis? It was the definitely insignificant
event of my friend giving me *a drive in a cab free of cost.*
The situation in the dream at the table d'hôte contained an

---

[2][This sentence is in spaced type in the original.]
[3][This last half of this sentence is in spaced type in the original.]

allusion to this insignificant precipitating cause, for in my conversation I had compared the taximeter cab with a table d'hôte. But I can also point to the important experience which was represented by this trivial one. A few days earlier I had paid out a considerable sum of money on behalf of a member of my family of whom I am fond. No wonder, said the dream thoughts, if this person were to feel grateful to me: love of that sort would not be "free of cost." Love that is free of cost, however, stood in the forefront of the dream thoughts. The fact that not long before I had had several *cab drives* with the relative in question, made it possible for the cab drive with my friend to remind me of my connections with this other person.

The indifferent impression which becomes a dream instigator owing to associations of this kind is subject to a further condition which does not apply to the true source of the dream: it must always be a *recent* impression, derived from the dream day.

I cannot leave the subject of dream displacement without drawing attention to a remarkable process which occurs in the formation of dreams and in which condensation and displacement *combine* to produce the result. In considering condensation we have already seen the way in which two ideas in the dream thoughts which have something in common, some point of contact, are replaced in the dream content by a composite idea, in which a relatively distinct nucleus represents what they have in common, while indistinct subordinate details correspond to the respects in which they differ from each other. If displacement takes place in addition to condensation, what is constructed is not a composite idea but an "intermediate common entity," which stands in a relation to the two different elements similar to that in which the resultant in a parallelogram of forces stands to its components. For instance, in the content of one of my dreams there was a question of an injection with *propyl*. To begin with, the analysis only led me to an indifferent experience which had acted as dream instigator, and in which a part was played by *amyl*. I was not yet able to justify the confusion between amyl and propyl. In the group of ideas behind this same dream, however, there was also a recollection of my first visit to Munich, where I had been struck by the *Propylaea*. [4] The details of the analysis made it plausible to suppose that it was the influence of this second group of ideas upon the first one that was responsible for the displacement from amyl to propyl. *Propyl* is, as it were, an intermediate idea between *amyl* and *Propylaea*, and found its way into the content of the dream as a kind of *compromise*, by means of simultaneous condensation and displacement. [5]

There is a still more urgent necessity in the case of the process of displacement than in that of condensation to discover the motive for these puzzling efforts on the part of the dream work.

---

[4] [A ceremonial portico on the Athenian model.]
[5] [The dream from which this detail is taken was the first one to be exhaustively analyzed by Freud. It is reported at length in *The Interpretation of Dreams* (1900), Chapter II.]

VI

It is the process of displacement which is chiefly responsible for our being unable to discover or recognize the dream thoughts in the dream content, unless we understand the reason for their distortion. Nevertheless, the dream thoughts are also submitted to another and milder sort of transformation, which leads to our discovering a new achievement on the part of the dream work—one, however, which is easily intelligible. The dream thoughts which we first come across as we proceed with our analysis often strike us by the unusual form in which they are expressed; they are not clothed in the prosaic language usually employed by our thoughts, but are on the contrary represented symbolically by means of similes and metaphors, in images resembling those of poetic speech. There is no difficulty in accounting for the constraint imposed upon the form in which the dream thoughts are expressed. The manifest content of dreams consists for the most part in pictorial situations; and the dream thoughts must accordingly be submitted in the first place to a treatment which will make them suitable for a representation of this kind. If we imagine ourselves faced by the problem of representing the arguments in a political leading article or the speeches of counsel before a court of law in a series of pictures, we shall easily understand the

modifications which must necessarily be carried out by the
dream work owing to *considerations of representability in the
content of the dream.*

The psychical material of the dream thoughts habitually
includes recollections of impressive experiences—not infrequently dating back to early childhood—which are thus
themselves perceived as a rule as situations having a visual
subject matter. Wherever the possibility arises, this portion
of the dream thoughts exercises a determining influence
upon the form taken by the content of the dream; it constitutes, as it were, a nucleus of crystallization, attracting the
material of the dream thoughts to itself and thus affecting
their distribution. The situation in a dream is often nothing
other than a modified repetition, complicated by interpolations, of an impressive experience of this kind; on the other
hand, faithful and straightforward reproductions of real
scenes only rarely appear in dreams.

The content of dreams, however, does not consist entirely
of situations, but also includes disconnected fragments of
visual images, speeches and even bits of unmodified
thoughts. It may, therefore, perhaps be of interest to enu-
merate very briefly the modes of representation available to
the dream work for reproducing the dream thoughts in the
peculiar form of expression necessary in dreams.

The dream thoughts which we arrive at by means of
analysis reveal themselves as a psychical complex of the most
intricate possible structure. Its portions stand in the most
manifold logical relations to one another: they represent
foreground and background, conditions, digressions and il-
lustrations, chains of evidence and counterarguments. Each
train of thought is almost invariably accompanied by its
contradictory counterpart. This material lacks none of the
characteristics that are familiar to us from our waking thinking. If now all of this is to be turned into a dream, the

psychical material will be submitted to a pressure which will condense it greatly, to an internal fragmentation and displacement which will, as it were, create new surfaces, and to a selective operation in favor of those portions of it which are the most appropriate for the construction of situations. If we take into account the genesis of the material, a process of this sort deserves to be described as a "regression." In the course of this transformation, however, the logical links which have hitherto held the psychical material together are lost. It is only, as it were, the substantive content of the dream thoughts that the dream work takes over and manipulates. The restoration of the connections which the dream work has destroyed is a task which has to be performed by the work of analysis.

The modes of expression open to a dream may therefore be qualified as meager by comparison with those of our intellectual speech; nevertheless a dream need not wholly abandon the possibility of reproducing the logical relations present in the dream thoughts. On the contrary, it succeeds often enough in replacing them by formal characteristics in its own texture.

In the first place, dreams take into account the connection which undeniably exists between all the portions of the dream thoughts by combining the whole material into a single situation. They reproduce *logical connection* by *approximation in time and space,* just as a painter will represent all the poets in a single group in a picture of Parnassus. It is true that they were never, in fact, assembled on a single mountaintop; but they certainly form a conceptual group. Dreams carry this method of reproduction down to details; and often when they show us two elements in the dream content close together, this indicates that there is some specially intimate connection between what correspond to them among the dream thoughts. Incidentally, it is to be observed that all dreams produced during a single night will be found on analysis to be derived from the same circle of thoughts.

A *casual relation* between two thoughts is either left unrepresented or is replaced by a *sequence* of two pieces of dream of different lengths. Here the representation is often reversed, the beginning of the dream standing for the consequence and its conclusion for the premise. An immediate *transformation* of one thing into another in a dream seems to represent the relation of *cause and effect.*

The alternative *"either—or"* is never expressed in dreams, both of the alternatives being inserted in the text of the dream as though they were equally valid. I have already mentioned that an "either—or" used in *recording* a dream is to be translated by "and." [See p. 28.]

Ideas which are contraries are by preference expressed in dreams by one and the same element.[1] "No" seems not to exist so far as dreams are concerned. Opposition between two thoughts, the relation of *reversal,* may be represented in dreams in a most remarkable way. It may be represented by some *other* piece of the dream content being turned into its opposite—as it were by an afterthought. We shall hear presently of a further method of expressing contradiction. The sensation of *inhibition of movement* which is so common in dreams also serves to express a contradiction between two impulses, a *conflict of will.*

One and one only of these logical relations—that of *similarity, consonance, the possession of common attributes*—is very highly favored by the mechanism of dream

---

[1][*Footnote added* 1911:] It deserves to be remarked that well-known philologists have asserted that the most ancient human languages tended in general to express contradictory opposites by the same word. (*E.g.,* "strong-weak," "inside-outside." This has been described as "the antithetical meaning of primal words.") [Cf. Freud, 1910.]

formation. The dream work makes use of such cases as a foundation for dream condensation, by bringing together everything that shows an agreement of this kind into a *new unity*.

This short series of rough comments is, of course, inadequate to deal with the full extent of the formal means employed by dreams for the expression of logical relations in the dream thoughts. Different dreams are more or less carefully constructed in this respect; they keep more or less closely to the text presented to them; they make more or less use of the expedients that are open to the dream work. In the second case, they appear obscure, confused and disconnected. If, however, a dream strikes one as *obviously* absurd, if its content includes a piece of palpable nonsense, this is intentionally so; its apparent disregard of all the requirements of logic is expressing a piece of the intellectual content of the dream thoughts. Absurdity in a dream signifies the presence in the dream thoughts of *contradiction, ridicule, and derision.* Since this statement is in the most marked opposition to the view that dreams are the product of a dissociated and uncritical mental activity, I will emphasize it by means of an example.

One of my acquaintances, Herr M., had been attacked in an essay with an unjustifiable degree of violence, as we all thought—by no less a person than Goethe. Herr M. was naturally crushed by the attack. He complained of it bitterly to some company at table; his veneration for Goethe had not been affected, however, by this personal experience. I now tried to throw a little light on the chronological data, which seemed to me improbable. Goethe died in 1832. Since his attack on Herr M. must naturally have been made earlier than that, Herr M. must have been quite a young man at the time. It seemed to be a plausible notion that he was eighteen. I was not quite sure, however, what year we were actually in, so that my whole calculation melted into obscurity. Incidentally, the attack was contained in Goethe's well-known essay on "Nature."

The nonsensical character of this dream will be even more glaringly obvious, if I explain that Herr M. is a youngish businessman, who is far removed from any poetical and literary interests. I have no doubt, however, that when I have entered into the analysis of the dream I shall succeed in showing how much "method" there is in its nonsense.

The material of the dream was derived from three sources:

(1) Herr M., whom I had got to know among some *company at table,* asked me one day to examine his elder brother, who was showing signs of general paralysis. In the course of my conversation with the patient an awkward episode occurred, for he gave his brother away for no accountable reason by talking of his *youthful follies.* I had asked the patient the *year of his birth* (cf. the *year of* Goethe's *death* in the dream) and had made him carry out a number of calculations in order to test the weakness of his memory.

(2) A medical journal, which bore my name among others on its title page, had published a positively *"crushing"* criticism by a *youthful* reviewer of a book by my friend F. in Berlin. I took the editor to task over this; but, though he expressed his regret, he would not undertake to offer any redress. I therefore severed my connection with the journal, but in my letter of resignation expressed a hope that *our personal relations would not be affected by the event.* This was the true source of the dream. The unfavorable reception of my friend's work had made a profound impression on me. It contained, in my opinion, a fundamental biological dis-

covery, which is only now—many years later—beginning to find favor with the experts.

(3) A woman patient of mine had given me an account a short time before of her brother's illness, and how he had broken out in a frenzy with cries of *"Nature! Nature!"* The doctors believed that this exclamation came from his having read *Goethe's* striking essay on that subject and that it showed he had been overworking at his studies. I had remarked that *it seemed to me more plausible* that his exclamation of the word "Nature" should be taken in the sexual sense in which it is used even by the less educated people here. This idea of mine was at least not disproved by the fact that the unfortunate young man subsequently mutilated his own genitals. He was *eighteen* at the time of his outbreak.

Behind my own ego in the dream content there lay concealed, in the first instance, my friend who had been so badly treated by the critic. *"I tried to throw a little light on the chronological data."* My friend's book dealt with the *chronological data* of life and among other things showed that the length of *Goethe's* life was a multiple of a number of days that has a significance in biology. But this ego was compared with a paralytic: *"I was not quite sure what year we were in."* Thus the dream made out that my friend was behaving like a paralytic, and in this respect it was a mass of absurdities. The dream thoughts, however, were saying ironically: "Naturally, it's *he* [my friend F.] who is the crazy fool and it's *you* [the critics] who are the men of genius and know better. Surely it couldn't be the *reverse?"* There were plenty of examples of this *reversal* in the dream. For instance, Goethe attacked the young man, which is absurd, whereas it is still easy for quite a young man to attack the great Goethe.

I should like to lay it down that no dream is prompted by

motives other than egoistic ones.[2] In fact, the ego in the present dream does not stand only for my friend but for myself as well. I was identifying myself with him, because the fate of his discovery seemed to foreshadow the reception of my own findings. If I were to bring forward my theory emphasizing the part played by sexuality in the etiology of psychoneurotic disorders (cf. the allusion to the eighteen-year-old patient's cry of "Nature! Nature!"), I should come across the same criticisms; and I was already preparing to meet them with the same derision.

If we pursue the dream thoughts further, we shall keep on finding ridicule and derision as correlates of the absurdities of the manifest dream. It is well known that it was the discovery of the split skull of a sheep on the Lido of Venice that gave Goethe the idea of the so-called "vertebral" theory of the skull. My friend boasts that, when he was a student, he released a storm which led to the resignation of an old Professor who, though he had once been distinguished (among other things in connection precisely with the same branch of comparative anatomy), had become incapable of teaching owing to *senile dementia.* Thus the agitation which my friend promoted served to combat the mischievous system according to which there is no *age limit* for academic workers in German universities for *age is proverbially no defense against folly.*

In the hospital here I had the honor of serving for years under a chief who had long been a *fossil* and had for decades been notoriously *feeble-minded,* but who was allowed to continue carrying on his responsible duties. At this point I thought of a descriptive term based upon the discovery on

---

[2][Freud has, however, qualified this statement in an additional footnote written in 1925, which will be found near the end of Chapter V of *The Interpretation of Dreams* (1900).]

the Lido.[3] Some of my young contemporaries at the hospital concocted, in connection with this man, a version of what was then a popular song: *"Das hat kein Goethe g'schrieben, das hat kein Schiller g'dicht . . ."*[4]

---

[3] [*"Schafkopf,"* literally "sheep's head"—"silly ass."]
[4] ["This was written by no Goethe, this was composed by no Schiller." This dream is also discussed at length in *The Interpretation of Dreams* (1900), Section G of Chapter VI.]

VII

We have not yet come to the end of our consideration of
the dream work. In addition to condensation, displacement,
and pictorial arrangement of the psychical material, we are
obliged to assign it yet another activity, though this is not
to be found in operation in *every* dream. I shall not deal
exhaustively with this part of the dream work, and will
therefore merely remark that the easiest way of forming an
idea of its nature is to suppose—though the supposition
probably does not meet the facts—that it only comes into
operation *after* the dream content has already been constructed. Its function would then consist in arranging the
constituents of the dream in such a way that they form an
approximately connected whole, a dream composition. In
this way the dream is given a kind of façade (though this
does not, it is true, hide its content at every point), and thus
receives a first, preliminary interpretation, which is sup-
ported by interpolations and slight modifications. Incidentally, this revision of the dream content is only possible if it
is not too punctiliously carried out; nor does it present us
with anything more than a glaring misunderstanding of the
dream thoughts. Before we start upon the analysis of a
dream we have to clear the ground of this attempt at an
interpretation.

The motive for this part of the dream work is particularly obvious. *Considerations of intelligibility* are what lead to this final revision of a dream; and this reveals the origin of the activity. It behaves toward the dream content lying before it just as our normal psychical activity behaves in general toward any perceptual content that may be presented to it. It understands that content on the basis of certain anticipatory ideas, and arranges it, even at the moment of perceiving it, on the presupposition of its being intelligible; in so doing it runs a risk of falsifying it, and in fact, if it cannot bring it into line with anything familiar, is a prey to the strangest misunderstandings. As is well known, we are incapable of seeing a series of unfamiliar signs or of hearing a succession of unknown words, without at once falsifying the perception from considerations of intelligibility, on the basis of something already known to us.

Dreams which have undergone a revision of this kind at the hands of a psychical activity completely analogous to waking thought may be described as "well-constructed." In the case of other dreams this activity has completely broken down; no attempt even has been made to arrange or interpret the material, and, since after we have waked up we feel ourselves identical with this last part of the dream work, we make a judgment that the dream was "hopelessly confused." From the point of view of analysis, however, a dream that resembles a disordered heap of disconnected fragments is just as valuable as one that has been beautifully polished and provided with a surface. In the former case, indeed, we are saved the trouble of demolishing what has been superimposed upon the dream content.

It would be a mistake, however, to suppose[1] that these dream façades are nothing other than mistaken and some-

---

[1] [This paragraph was added in 1911.]

what arbitrary revisions of the dream content by the conscious agency of our mental life. In the erection of a dream
façade use is not infrequently made of wishful fantasies
which are present in the dream thoughts in a preconstructed
form, and are of the same character as the appropriately
named "daydreams" familiar to us in waking life. The wishful fantasies revealed by analysis in night dreams often turn
out to be repetitions or modified versions of scenes from
infancy; thus in some cases the façade of the dream directly
reveals the dream's actual nucleus, distorted by an admix-
ture of other material.

The dream work exhibits no activities other than the four
that have already been mentioned. If we keep to the definition of "dream work" as the process of transforming the
dream thoughts into the dream content, it follows that the
dream work is not creative, that it develops no fantasies of
its own, that it makes no judgments and draws no conclusions; it has no functions whatever other than condensation
and displacement of the material and its modification into
pictorial form, to which must be added as a variable factor
the final bit of interpretative revision. It is true that we find
various things in the dream content which we should be
inclined to regard as a product of some other and higher
intellectual function; but in every case analysis shows con-
vincingly that these intellectual operations have already
been performed in the dream thoughts and have only been
taken over by the dream content.[2] A conclusion drawn in
a dream is nothing other than the repetition of a conclusion
in the dream thoughts; if the conclusion is taken over into
the dream unmodified, it will appear impeccable; if the
dream work has displaced it on to some other material, it will
appear nonsensical. A calculation in the dream content sig-

---

[2][The last clause is in spaced type in the original.]

nifies nothing more than that there is a calculation in the dream thoughts; but while the latter is always rational, a dream calculation may produce the wildest results if its factors are condensed or if its mathematical operations are displaced on to other material. Not even the speeches that occur in the dream content are original compositions; they turn out to be a hotchpotch of speeches made, heard, or read, which have been revived in the dream thoughts and whose wording is exactly reproduced, while their origin is entirely disregarded and their meaning is violently changed.

It will perhaps be as well to support these last assertions by a few examples.

(I) Here is an innocent-sounding, well-constructed dream dreamed by a woman patient:

> She dreamed she was going to the market with her cook, who was carrying the basket. After she had asked for something, the butcher said to her, "That's not obtainable any longer," and offered her something else, adding, "This is good too." She rejected it and went on to the woman who sells vegetables, who tried to get her to buy a peculiar vegetable that was tied up in bundles but was of a black color. She said, "I don't recognize that. I won't take it."

The remark *"That's not obtainable any longer"* originated from the treatment itself. A few days earlier I had explained to the patient in those very words that the earliest memories of childhood were *"not obtainable any longer* as such," but were replaced in analysis by "transferences" and dreams. So *I* was the butcher.

The second speech—*"I don't recognize that"*—occurred in an entirely different connection. On the previous day she had reproved her cook, who incidentally also appeared in the dream, with the words, *"Behave yourself properly! I don't*

recognize that!"—meaning, no doubt, that she did not understand such behavior and would not put up with it. As the
result of a displacement, it was the more innocent part of
this speech which made its way into the content of the
dream; but in the dream thoughts it was only the other part
of the speech that played a part. For the dream work had
reduced to complete unintelligibility and extreme innocence
an imaginary situation in which *I* was *behaving improperly*
to the lady in a particular way. But this situation which the
patient was expecting in her imagination was itself only a
new edition of something she had once actually experi-
enced.[3]

(II) Here is an apparently quite meaningless dream con-
taining figures.

> She was going to pay for something. Her daughter took
> 3 florins and 65 kreuzers from her (the mother's) purse. The
> dreamer said to her, "What are you about? It only costs 21
> kreuzers."

The dreamer came from abroad and her daughter was at
school here. She was in a position to carry on her treatment
with me as long as her daughter remained in Vienna. The
day before the dream the headmistress had suggested to her
that she should leave her daughter at school for another year.
In that case she could also have continued her treatment for
a year. The figures in the dream become significant if we
remember that "time is money." One year is equal to 365
days, or, expressed in money, 365 kreuzers or 3 florins 65
kreuzers. The 21 kreuzers corresponded to the 3 weeks
which had still to run between the dream day and the end

---

[3][This dream is reported in greater detail in *The Interpretation of Dreams*
(1900), Chapter V, Section A.]

of the school term and also to the end of the patient's treatment. It was clearly financial considerations which had induced the lady to refuse the headmistress's proposal, and which were responsible for the smallness of the sums mentioned in the dream.[4]

(III) A lady who, though she was still young, had been married for a number of years, received news that an acquaintance of hers, Fräulein Elise L., who was almost exactly her contemporary, had become engaged. This was the precipitating cause of the following dream:

> She was at the theater with her husband. One side of the stalls was completely empty. Her husband told her that Elise L. and her fiancé had wanted to go too, but had only been able to get bad seats—three for 1 florin 50 kreuzers—and of course they could not take those. She thought it would not really have done any harm if they had.

What interests us here is the source of the figures in the material of the dream thoughts and the transformations which they underwent. What was the origin of the 1 florin 50 kreuzers? It came from what was, in fact, an indifferent event of the previous day. Her sister-in-law had been given a present of 150 florins by her husband and had *been in a hurry* to get rid of them by buying a piece of jewelry. It is to be noticed that 150 florins is a *hundred* times as much as 1 florin 50 kreuzers. The only connection with the "three," which was the number of the theater tickets, was that her newly engaged friend was that number of months— three—her junior. The situation in the dream was a repetition of a small incident which her husband often teased her

---

[4][For this dream see *The Interpretation of Dreams* (1900), Chapter VI, Section F. An Austrian florin was worth approximately 1s. 10d or 40 cents at the end of the nineteenth century.]

about. On one occasion she had been in a great hurry to buy
tickets for a play in advance, and when she got to the theater
she had found that one side of the stalls was almost completely empty. There had been *no need for her to be in such
a hurry*. Finally, we must not overlook the *absurdity* in the
dream of two people taking three tickets for a play.

Now for the dream thoughts: "It was *absurd* to marry so
early. There was *no need for me to be in such a hurry*. I see
from Elise L.'s example that I should have got a husband in
the end. Indeed, I should have got one *a hundred times
better*" (a treasure) "if I had only waited. My money" (or
dowry) "could have bought *three* men just as good."[5]

---

[5][This dream, which is mentioned again below, on p. 58 is discussed in
Chapter VI, Section F of *The Interpretation of Dreams* (1900) and at
greater length in Freud's *Introductory Lectures* (1916–17), especially in
Lectures VII and XIV.]

VIII

Having been made acquainted with the dream work by the foregoing discussion, we shall no doubt be inclined to pronounce it a quite peculiar psychical process, the like of which, so far as we are aware, does not exist elsewhere. It is as though we were carrying over on to the dream work all the astonishment which used formerly to be aroused in us by its product, the dream. In fact, however, the dream work is only the first to be discovered of a whole series of psychical processes, responsible for the generation of hysterical symptoms, of phobias, obsessions and delusions. Condensation and, above all, displacement are invariable characteristics of these other processes as well. Modification into a pictorial form, on the other hand, remains a peculiarity of the dream work. If this explanation places dreams in a single series alongside the structures produced by psychical illness, this makes it all the more important for us to discover the essential determining conditions of such processes as those of dream formation. We shall probably be surprised to hear that neither the state of sleep nor illness is among these indispensable conditions. A whole number of the phenomena of the everyday life of healthy people—such as forgetting, slips of the tongue, bungled actions and a particular class of errors—owe their origin to a psychical mechanism analogous to that of dreams and of the other members of the series.[1]

The heart of the problem lies in displacement, which is by far the most striking of the special achievements of the dream work. If we enter deeply into the subject, we come to realize that the essential determining condition of displacement is a purely psychological one: something in the nature of a *motive*. One comes upon its track if one takes into consideration certain experiences which one cannot escape in analyzing dreams. In analyzing my specimen dream I was obliged to break off my report of the dream thoughts on page 15, because, as I confessed, there were some among them which I should prefer to conceal from strangers and which I could not communicate to other people without doing serious mischief in important directions. I added that nothing would be gained if I were to choose another dream instead of that particular one with a view to reporting its analysis: I should come upon dream thoughts which required to be kept secret in the case of *every* dream with an obscure or confused content. If, however, I were to continue the analysis on my own account, without any reference to other people (whom, indeed, an experience so personal as my dream cannot possibly have been intended to reach), I should eventually arrive at thoughts which would surprise me, whose presence in me I was unaware of, which were not only *alien* but also *disagreeable* to me, and which I should, therefore, feel inclined to dispute energetically, although the chain of thoughts running through the analysis insisted upon them remorselessly. There is only one way of accounting for this state of affairs, which is of quite universal occurrence; and that is to suppose that these thoughts really were present in my mind, and in possession of a certain

---

[1][See Freud's *Psychopathology of Everyday Life* (1901).]

amount of psychical intensity or energy, but that they were in a peculiar psychological situation, as a consequence of which they *could not become conscious* to me. (I describe this particular condition as one of "repression.") We cannot help concluding, then, that there is a causal connection between the obscurity of the dream content and the state of repression (inadmissibility to consciousness) of certain of the dream thoughts, and that the dream had to be obscure so as not to betray the proscribed dream thoughts. Thus we are led to the concept of a "dream distortion," which is the product of the dream work and serves the purpose of dissimulation, that is, of disguise.

I will test this on the specimen dream which I chose for analysis, and inquire what the thought was which made its way into that dream in a distorted form, and which I should be inclined to repudiate if it were undistorted. I recall that my free cab drive reminded me of my recent expensive drive with a member of my family, that the interpretation of the dream was "I wish I might for once experience love that cost me nothing," and that a short time before the dream I had been obliged to spend a considerable sum of money on this same person's account. Bearing this context in mind, I cannot escape the conclusion that *I regret having made that expenditure.* Not until I have recognized this impulse does my wish in the dream for the love which would call for *no* expenditure acquire a meaning. Yet I can honestly say that when I decided to spend this sum of money I did not hesitate for a moment. My regret at having to do so—the contrary current of feeling—did not become conscious to me. *Why* it did not, is another and a far-reaching question, the answer to which is known to me but belongs in another connection.

If the dream that I analyze is not my own, but someone else's, the conclusion will be the same, though the grounds for believing it will be different. If the dreamer is a healthy person, there is no other means open to me of obliging him to recognize the repressed ideas that have been discovered than by pointing out the context of the dream thoughts; and I cannot help it if he refuses to recognize them. If, however, I am dealing with a neurotic patient, with a hysteric, for instance, he will find the acceptance of the repressed thought forced upon him, owing to its connection with the symptoms of his illness, and owing to the improvement he experiences when he exchanges those symptoms for the repressed ideas. In the case, for instance, of the woman patient who had the dream I have just quoted about the three theater tickets which cost 1 florin 50 kreuzers, the analysis led to the inevitable conclusion that she had a low estimate of her husband (cf. her idea that she could have got one "a hundred times better"), that she regretted having married him, and that she would have liked to exchange him for another one. It is true that she asserted that she loved her husband, and that her emotional life knew nothing of any such low estimate of him, but all her symptoms led to the same conclusion as the dream. And after her repressed memories had been revived of a particular period during which she had consciously not loved her husband, her symptoms cleared up and her resistance against the interpretation of the dream disappeared.

IX

Now that we have established the concept of repression and have brought dream distortion into relation with repressed psychical material, we can express in general terms the principal finding to which we have been led by the analysis of dreams. In the case of dreams which are intelligible and have a meaning, we have found that they are undisguised wish fulfillments; that is, that in their case the dream situation represents as fulfilled a wish which is known to consciousness, which is left over from daytime life, and which is deservedly of interest. Analysis has taught us something entirely analogous in the case of obscure and confused dreams: once again the dream situation represents a wish as fulfilled—a wish which invariably arises from the dream thoughts, but one which is represented in an unrecognizable form and can only be explained when it has been traced back in analysis. The wish in such cases is either itself a repressed one and alien to consciousness, or it is intimately connected with repressed thoughts and is based upon them. Thus the formula for such dreams is as follows: they are disguised fulfillments of repressed wishes.[1] It is interesting in this connection to observe that the popular belief that dreams

---

[1] [The last clause is in spaced type in the original.]

always foretell the future is confirmed. Actually, the future which the dream shows us is not the one which *will* occur but the one which we should *like* to occur. The popular mind is behaving here as it usually does: what it believes is what it wishes.

Dreams fall into three classes according to their attitude to wish fulfillment. The first class consists of those which represent an unrepressed wish undisguisedly; these are the dreams of an infantile type which become ever rarer in adults. Secondly, there are the dreams which express a repressed wish disguisedly; these no doubt form the overwhelming majority of all our dreams, and require analysis before they can be understood. In the third place, there are the dreams which represent a repressed wish, but do so with insufficient or no disguise. These last dreams are invariably accompanied by anxiety, which interrupts them. In their case anxiety takes the place of dream distortion; and, in dreams of the second class, anxiety is only avoided owing to the dream work. There is no great difficulty in proving that the ideational content which produces anxiety in us in dreams was once a wish but has since undergone repression.

There are also clear dreams with a distressing content, which, however, is not felt as distressing in the dream itself. For this reason they cannot be counted as anxiety dreams; but they have always been taken as evidence of the fact that dreams are without meaning and have no psychical value. An analysis of a dream of this kind will show that we are dealing with well-disguised fulfillments of repressed wishes, that is to say with a dream of the second class; it will also show how admirably the process of displacement is adapted for disguising wishes.

A girl had a dream of seeing her sister's only surviving child lying dead in the same surroundings in which a few years earlier she had, in fact, seen the dead body of her sister's *first* child. She felt no pain over this; but she naturally rejected the idea that this situation represented any wish of hers. Nor was there any need to suppose this. It had been beside the first child's coffin, however, that, years before, she had seen and spoken to the man she was in love with; if the second child died, she would no doubt meet the man again in her sister's house. She longed for such a meeting, but fought against the feeling. On the dream day she had bought a ticket for a lecture which was to be given by this same man, to whom she was still devoted. Her dream was a simple dream of impatience of the kind that often occurs before journeys, visits to the theater, and similar enjoyments that lie ahead. But in order to disguise this longing from her, the situation was displaced on to an event of a kind most unsuitable for producing a feeling of enjoyment, though it had in fact done so in the past. It is to be observed that the emotional behavior in the dream was appropriate to the real content which lay in the background and not to what was pushed into the foreground. The dream situation antici-pated the meeting she had so long desired; it offered no basis for any painful feelings.[2]

---

[2][This dream is reported in greater detail in *The Interpretation of Dreams* (1900), Chapter IV.]

X

Hitherto philosophers have had no occasion to concern themselves with a psychology of repression. We may therefore be permitted to make a first approach to this hitherto unknown topic by constructing a pictorial image of the course of events in dream formation. It is true that the schematic picture we have arrived at—not only from the study of dreams—is a fairly complicated one; but we cannot manage with anything simpler. Our hypothesis is that in our mental apparatus there are two thought-constructing agencies, of which the second enjoys the privilege of having free access to consciousness for its products, whereas the activity of the first is in itself unconscious and can only reach consciousness by way of the second. On the frontier between the two agencies, where the first passes over to the second, there is a censorship, which only allows what is agreeable to it to pass through and holds back everything else. According to our definition, then, what is rejected by the censorship is in a state of repression. Under certain conditions, of which the state of sleep is one, the relation between the strength of the two agencies is modified in such a way that what is repressed can no longer be held back. In the state of sleep this probably occurs owing to a relaxation of the censorship; when this happens it becomes possible for what has hitherto been repressed to make a path for itself to consciousness. Since, however, the censorship is never completely eliminated but merely reduced, the repressed material must submit to certain alterations which mitigate its offensive features. What becomes conscious in such cases is a compromise between the intentions of one agency and the demands of the other. *Repression—relaxation of the censorship—the formation of a compromise,* this is the fundamental pattern for the generation not only of dreams but of many other psychopathological structures; and in the latter cases, too, we may observe that the formation of compromises is accompanied by processes of condensation and displacement and by the employment of superficial associations, which we have become familiar with in the dream work.

We have no reason to disguise the fact that in the hypothesis which we have set up in order to explain the dream work a part is played by what might be described as a "demonic" element. We have gathered an impression that the formation of obscure dreams occurs *as though* one person who was dependent upon a second person had to make a remark which was bound to be disagreeable in the ears of this second one; and it is on the basis of this simile that we have arrived at the concepts of dream distortion and censorship, and have endeavored to translate our impression into a psychological theory which is no doubt crude but is at least lucid. Whatever it may be with which a further investigation of the subject may enable us to identify our first and second agencies, we may safely expect to find a confirmation of some correlate of our hypothesis that the second agency controls access to consciousness and can bar the first agency from such access.

When the state of sleep is over, the censorship quickly recovers its full strength; and it can now wipe out all that was won from it during the period of its weakness. This must be one part at least of the explanation of the forgetting of dreams, as is shown by an observation which has been confirmed on countless occasions. It not infrequently happens that during the narration of a dream or during its analysis a fragment of the dream content which had seemed to be forgotten re-emerges. This fragment which has been rescued from oblivion invariably affords us the best and most direct access to the meaning of the dream. And that, in all probability, must have been the only reason for its having been forgotten, that is, for its having been once more suppressed.

XI

When once we have recognized that the content of a dream is the representation of a fulfilled wish and that its obscurity is due to alterations in repressed material made by the censorship, we shall no longer have any difficulty in discovering the *function* of dreams. It is commonly said that sleep is disturbed by dreams; strangely enough, we are led to a contrary view and must regard dreams as *the guardians of sleep*.

In the case of children's dreams there should be no difficulty in accepting this statement. The state of sleep or the psychical modification involved in sleep, whatever that may be, is brought about by a resolve to sleep which is either imposed upon the child or is reached on the basis of sensations of fatigue; and it is only made possible by the withholding of stimuli which might suggest to the psychical apparatus aims other than that of sleeping. The means by which *external* stimuli can be kept off are familiar to us; but what are the means available for controlling *internal* mental stimuli which set themselves against falling asleep? Let us observe a mother putting her child to sleep. The child gives vent to an unceasing stream of desires: he wants one more kiss, he wants to go on playing. His mother satisfies some of these desires, but uses her authority to postpone others of them to the next day. It is clear that any wishes or needs that may arise have an inhibiting effect upon falling asleep. We all know the amusing story told by Balduin Groller [a popular 19th century German novelist] of the bad little boy who woke in the night and shouted across the night nursery: "I want the rhino!" A better behaved child, instead of shouting, would have *dreamed* that he was playing with the rhino. Since a dream that shows a wish as fulfilled is *believed* during sleep, it does away with the wish and makes sleep possible. It cannot be disputed that dream images are believed in in this way, for they are clothed in the psychical appearance of perceptions, and children have not yet acquired the later faculty of distinguishing hallucinations or fantasies from reality.

Adults have learned to make this distinction; they have also grasped the uselessness of wishing, and after long practice know how to postpone their desires until they can find satisfaction by the long and roundabout path of altering the external world. In their case, accordingly, wish fulfillments along the short psychical path are rare in sleep too; it is even possible, indeed, that they never occur at all, and that anything that may seem to us to be constructed on the pattern of a child's dream in fact requires a far more complicated solution. On the other hand, in the case of adults—and this no doubt applies without exception to everyone in full possession of his senses—a differentiation has occurred in the psychical material, which was not present in children. A psychical agency has come into being, which, taught by experience of life, exercises a dominating and inhibiting influence upon mental impulses and maintains that influence with jealous severity, and which, owing to its relation to consciousness and to intentional movement, is armed with the strongest instruments of psychical power. A portion of the impulses of childhood has been suppressed by this agency as being useless to life, and any material of thought derived from those impulses is in a state of repression.

Now while this agency, in which we recognize our normal ego, is concentrated on the wish to sleep, it appears to be compelled by the psycho-physiological conditions of sleep to relax the energy with which it is accustomed to hold down the repressed material during the day. In itself, no doubt, this relaxation does no harm; however much the suppressed impulses of the childish mind may make a stir, their access to consciousness is still difficult and their access to movement is barred, as the result of this same state of sleep. The danger of sleep being disturbed by them must, however, be guarded against. We must in any case suppose that even during deep sleep a certain amount of free attention is on duty as a guard against sensory stimuli, and that this guard may sometimes consider waking more advisable than a continuation of sleep. Otherwise there would be no explanation of how it is that we can be waked up at any moment by sensory stimuli of some particular *quality*. As the physiologist Burdach [1838, 486] insisted long ago, a mother, for instance, will be roused by the whimpering of her baby, or a miller if his mill comes to a stop, or most people if they are called softly by their own name. Now the attention which is thus on guard is also directed toward internal wishful stimuli arising from the repressed material, and combines with them to form the dream which, as a compromise, simultaneously satisfies both of the two agencies. The dream provides a kind of psychical consummation for the wish that has been suppressed (or formed with the help of repressed material) by representing it as fulfilled; but it also satisfies the other agency by allowing sleep to continue. In this respect our ego is ready to behave like a child; it gives credence to the dream images, as though what it wanted to say was: "Yes, yes! you're quite right, but let me go on sleeping!" The low estimate which we form of dreams when we are awake, and which we relate to their confused and apparently illogical character, is probably nothing other than the judgment passed by our sleeping ego upon the repressed impulses, a judgment based, with better right, upon the motor impotence of these disturbers of sleep. We are sometimes aware in our sleep of this contemptuous judgment. If the content of a dream goes too far in overstepping the censorship, we think: "After all, it's only a dream!"—and go on sleeping.

This view is not traversed by the fact that there are marginal cases in which the dream—as happens with anxiety dreams—can no longer perform its function of preventing an interruption of sleep, but assumes instead the other function of promptly bringing sleep to an end. In doing so it is merely behaving like a conscientious night watchman, who first carries out his duty by suppressing disturbances so that the townsmen may not be waked up, but afterward continues to do his duty by himself waking the townsmen up, if the causes of the disturbance seem to him serious and of a kind that he cannot cope with alone.

The function of the dream as a guardian of sleep becomes particularly evident when an external stimulus impinges upon the senses of a sleeper. It is generally recognized that sensory stimuli arising during sleep influence the content of dreams; this can be proved experimentally and is among the few certain (but, incidentally, greatly overvalued) findings of medical investigation into dreams. But this finding involves a puzzle which has hitherto proved insoluble. For the sensory stimulus which the experimenter causes to impinge upon the sleeper is not correctly recognized in the dream; it is subjected to one of an indefinite number of possible interpretations, the choice being apparently left to an arbi-

trary psychical determination. There is, of course, no such
thing as arbitrary determination in the mind. There are
several ways in which a sleeper may react to an external
sensory stimulus. He may wake up or he may succeed in
continuing his sleep in spite of it. In the latter case he may
make use of a dream in order to get rid of the external
stimulus, and here again there is more than one method
open to him. For instance, he may get rid of the stimulus
by dreaming that he is in a situation which is absolutely
incompatible with the stimulus. Such was the line taken by
a sleeper who was subject to disturbance by a painful abscess
on the perineum. He dreamed that he was riding on a horse,
making use of the poultice that was intended to mitigate his
pain as a saddle, and in this way he avoided being disturbed.[1]
Or, as happens more frequently, the external stimulus is
given an interpretation which brings it into the context of
a repressed wish which is at the moment awaiting fulfillment; in this way the external stimulus is robbed of its reality
and is treated as though it were a portion of the psychical
material. Thus someone dreamed that he had written a
comedy with a particular plot; it was produced in a theater,
the first act was over, and there were thunders of applause;
the clapping was terrific. . . . The dreamer must have succeeded in prolonging his sleep till after the interference had
ceased; for when he woke up he no longer heard the noise,
but rightly concluded that someone must have been beating
a carpet or mattress. Every dream which occurs immediately
before the sleeper is waked by a loud noise has made an
attempt at explaining away the arousing stimulus by provid-
ing another explanation of it and has thus sought to prolong
sleep, even if only for a moment.

---

[1][This dream is reported in full in *The Interpretation of Dreams* (1900),
Chapter V, Section C.]

XII

No one who accepts the view that the censorship is the chief
reason for dream distortion will be surprised to learn from
the results of dream interpretation that most of the dreams
of adults are traced back by analysis to *erotic wishes*. This
assertion is not aimed at dreams with an *undisguised* sexual
content, which are no doubt familiar to all dreamers from
their own experience and are as a rule the only ones to be
described as "sexual dreams." Even dreams of this latter
kind offer enough surprises in their choice of the people
whom they make into sexual objects, in their disregard of all
the limitations which the dreamer imposes in his waking life
upon his sexual desires, and by their many strange details,
hinting at what are commonly known as "perversions." A
great many other dreams, however, which show no sign of
being erotic in their manifest content, are revealed by the
work of interpretation in analysis as sexual wish fulfillments;
and, on the other hand, analysis proves that a great many
of the thoughts left over from the activity of waking life as
"residues of the previous day" only find their way to representation in dreams through the assistance of repressed
erotic wishes.

---

[1][The whole of this section was added in 1911.]

There is no theoretical necessity why this should be so; but to explain the fact it may be pointed out that no other group of instincts has been submitted to such far-reaching suppression by the demands of cultural education, while at the same time the sexual instincts are also the ones which, in most people, find it easiest to escape from the control of the highest mental agencies. Since we have become acquainted with infantile sexuality, which is often so unobtrusive in its manifestations and is always overlooked and misunderstood, we are justified in saying that almost every civilized man retains the infantile forms of sexual life in some respect or other. We can thus understand how it is that repressed infantile sexual wishes provide the most frequent and strongest motive forces for the construction of dreams.[2]

There is only one method by which a dream which expresses erotic wishes can succeed in appearing innocently nonsexual in its manifest content. The material of the sexual ideas must not be represented as such, but must be replaced in the content of the dream by hints, allusions and similar forms of indirect representation. But, unlike other forms of indirect representation, that which is employed in dreams must not be immediately intelligible. The modes of representation which fulfill these conditions are usually described as "symbols" of the things which they represent. Particular interest has been directed to them since it has been noticed that dreamers speaking the same language make use of the same symbols, and that in some cases, indeed, the use of the same symbols extends beyond the use of the same language. Since dreamers themselves are unaware of the meaning of the symbols they use, it is difficult at first sight to discover the source of the connection between the symbols and what

---

[2]See my *Three Essays on the Theory of Sexuality* (1905).

they replace and represent. The fact itself, however, is beyond doubt, and it is important for the technique of dream interpretation. For, with the help of a knowledge of dream symbolism, it is possible to understand the meaning of separate elements of the content of a dream or separate pieces of a dream or in some cases even whole dreams, without having to ask the dreamer for his associations. Here we are approaching the popular ideal of translating dreams and on the other hand are returning to the technique of interpretation used by the ancients, to whom dream interpretation was identical with interpretation by means of symbols.

Although the study of dream symbols is far from being complete, we are in a position to lay down with certainty a number of general statements and a quantity of special information on the subject. There are some symbols which bear a single meaning almost universally: thus the Emperor and Empress (or the King and Queen) stand for the parents, rooms represent women[3] and their entrances and exits the openings of the body. The majority of dream symbols serve to represent persons, parts of the body and activities invested with erotic interest; in particular, the genitals are represented by a number of often very surprising symbols, and the greatest variety of objects are employed to denote them symbolically. Sharp weapons, long and stiff objects, such as tree trunks and sticks, stand for the male genital; while cupboards, boxes, carriages or ovens may represent the uterus. In such cases as these the *tertium comparationis*, the common element in these substitutions, is immediately intelligible; but there are other symbols in which it is not so easy to grasp the connection. Symbols such as a staircase or

---

[3]Cf. *"Frauenzimmer"* [literally "women's apartment," commonly used in German as a slightly derogatory word for "woman."]

going upstairs, representing sexual intercourse, a tie or cravat for the male organ, or wood for the female one, provoke our unbelief until we can arrive at an understanding of the symbolic relation underlying them by some other means. Moreover a whole number of dream symbols are bisexual and can relate to the male or female genitals according to the context.

Some symbols are universally disseminated and can be met with in all dreamers belonging to a single linguistic or cultural group; there are others which occur only within the most restricted and individual limits, symbols constructed by an individual out of his own ideational material. Of the former class we can distinguish some whose claim to represent sexual ideas is immediately justified by linguistic usage (such, for instance, as those derived from agriculture, *e.g.* "fertilization" or "seed") and others whose relation to sexual ideas appears to reach back into the very earliest ages and to the most obscure depths of our conceptual functioning. The power of constructing symbols has not been exhausted in our own days in the case of either of the two sorts of symbols which I have distinguished at the beginning of this paragraph. Newly discovered objects (such as airships) are, as we may observe, at once adopted as universally available sexual symbols.

It would, incidentally, be a mistake to expect that if we had a still profounder knowledge of dream symbolism (of the "language of dreams") we could do without asking the dreamer for his associations to the dream and go back entirely to the technique of dream interpretation of antiquity. Quite apart from individual symbols and oscillations in the use of universal ones, one can never tell whether any particular element in the content of a dream is to be interpreted symbolically or in its proper sense, and one can be certain that the *whole* content of a dream is not to be interpreted symbolically. A knowledge of dream symbolism will never do more than enable us to translate certain constituents of the dream content, and will not relieve us of the necessity for applying the technical rules which I gave earlier. It will, however, afford the most valuable assistance to interpretation precisely at points at which the dreamer's associations are insufficient or fail altogether.

Dream symbolism is also indispensable to an understanding of what are known as "typical" dreams, which are common to everyone, and of "recurrent" dreams in individuals.

If the account I have given in this short discussion of the symbolic mode of expression in dreams appears incomplete, I can justify my neglect by drawing attention to one of the most important pieces of knowledge that we possess on this subject. Dream symbolism extends far beyond dreams: it is not peculiar to dreams, but exercises a similar dominating influence on representation in fairy tales, myths and legends, in jokes and in folklore. It enables us to trace the intimate connections between dreams and these latter productions. We must not suppose that dream symbolism is a creation of the dream work; it is in all probability a characteristic of the unconscious thinking which provides the dream work with the material for condensation, displacement and dramatization.[4]

---

[4]Further information on dream symbolism may be found in the works of early writers on dream interpretation, *e.g.* Artemidorus of Daldis and Scherner (1861), and also in my own *The Interpretation of Dreams* (1900) [Chapter VI, Section E], in the mythological studies of the psychoanalytic school, as well as in some of W. Stekel's writings (*e.g.* 1911). [See further Lecture X (on "Symbolism in Dreams") in Freud's *Introductory Lectures* (1916–17).]

XIII

I lay no claim to having thrown light in these pages upon *all* the problems of dreams, nor to having dealt in a convincing way with those that I *have* discussed. Anyone who is interested in the whole extent of the literature of dreams may be referred to a work by Sante de Sanctis (*I sogni*, 1899); and anyone who wishes to hear more detailed arguments in favor of the view of dreams which I myself have put forward should turn to my volume *The Interpretation of Dreams*, 1900.[1] It only remains for me now to indicate the direction in which my exposition of the subject of the dream work calls for pursuit.

I have laid it down as the task of dream interpretation to replace the dream by the latent dream thoughts, that is, to unravel what the dream work has woven. In so doing I have raised a number of new psychological problems dealing with the mechanism of this dream work itself, as well as with the nature and conditions of what is described as repression; on the other hand I have asserted the existence of the dream thoughts—a copious store of psychical structures of the highest order, which is characterized by all the signs of

---

[1][Cf. also the eleven lectures on dreams which constitute Part II of Freud's *Introductory Lectures* (1916–17).]

normal intellectual functioning, but is nevertheless with-drawn from consciousness till it emerges in distorted form in the dream content. I cannot but assume that thoughts of this kind are present in everyone, since almost everyone, including the most normal people, is capable of dreaming. The unconscious material of the dream thoughts and its relation to consciousness and to repression raise further questions of significance to psychology, the answers to which must no doubt be postponed until analysis has clarified the origin of other psychopathological structures, such as hyster-ical symptoms and obsessional ideas.

REFERENCES

ARTEMIDORUS OF DALDIS. *Oneirocritica.* (Translation by R. Wood, *The Interpretation of Dreames, London,* 1644.)

BINZ, C. (1878). *Über den Traum,* Bonn.

BURDACH, K. F. (1838). *Die Physiologie als Erfahrungswissenschaft,* Vol. 3, Leipzig (2d ed).

FREUD, S. (1900). (Translation.) *The Interpretation of Dreams,* Revised Ed., London, 1932.

FREUD, S. (1901). *Zur Psychopathologie des Alltagslebens,* Vienna.

FREUD, S. (1905). (Translation.) *Three Essays on the Theory of Sexuality,* London, 1949.

FREUD, S. (1910). (Translation.) "The Antithetical Sense of Primal Words," *Collected Papers,* Vol. 4, p. 184, London, 1925.

FREUD, S. (1916–17). (Translation.) *Introductory Lectures on Psycho-Analysis,* Revised Ed., London, 1929.

SANCTIS, S. de (1899). *I sogni,* Turin.

SCHERNER, K. A. (1861). *Das Leben des Traumes,* Berlin.

SCHUBERT, G. H. (1814). *Die Symbolik des Traumes,* Bamberg.

STEKEL, W. (1911). *Die Sprache des Traumes,* Wiesbaden.

STRÜMPELL, L. (1874). *Die Natur und Entstehung der Träume,* Leipzig.

VOLKELT, J. (1875). *Die Traum-Phantasie,* Stuttgart.

INDEX